BOSTON

BONECHI

Archeological excavations have revealed human settlements in Massachusetts dating to about 3000 years ago. The Algonquian-speaking tribes that inhabited the peninsula today occupied by the city of Boston called it Shawmut, or "where to find boats." The indigenous population was all but exterminated by the diseases transmitted by the first European explorers, who began to visit this part of the Atlantic coast in the 16th century.

The first European settlements in the Massachusetts Bay area date to about 1630, when Puritans fleeing persecution in England began to settle here: in particular, the large group led by John Winthrop, who in 1629 had obtained an independent colony charter from the English Crown and set up a self-governing permanent settlement. Boston took its name from Boston in Lincolnshire, former home of many of the immigrants; the name ultimately derives from Saint Botolph (from the O.E. bot = boat and ulph = helper), patron saint of fishermen and of the English town. The very first name given the colonial village was, however, Trimountain, from the three hills that dominated the peninsula: Mount Pemberton, Mount Vernon, and Beacon Hill. Only the last of the three remains, although greatly reduced: the others were leveled and became landfill for the mud flats and salt marshes along the shore in the 19th century. The area of the peninsula is, in fact, now triple that of 1630, and Boston's expansion is generally considered one of the greatest engineering feats in American history.

BOSTON: DER BEGINN

Laut archäologischen Ausgrabungen war Massachusetts schon vor 3000 Jahren besiedelt. Die Algonkin sprechenden Indianerstämme, die auf dem Gebiet des heutigen Boston wohnten, nannten die Halbinsel Shawmut, d.h. "wo man Boote findet." Die Eingeborenen wurden von den Krankheiten, die die ersten europäischen Entdecker im 16. Jh. einschleppten, fast vollständig dahingerafft. Die frühesten europäischen Siedlungen im Gebiet der Massachusetts Bay erfolgten etwa 1630, als sich in England verfolgte Puritaner hier niederließen, insbesondere eine große Gruppe unter der Führung von John Winthrop, welcher 1629 einen Freibrief für eine unabhängige Kolonie von der englischen Krone erhalten hatte und hier eine sich selbst verwaltende Ansiedlung gründete. Boston heißt nach Boston in Lincolnshire, der Heimat von vielen dieser Einwanderer. Ursprünglich stammte der Name von dem Hl. Botolph ab (im Altenglischen bot = boat und ulph = Helfer), Schutzpatron der Fischer und der englischen Stadt. Der allererste Namen des Kolonialdorfes lautete jedoch Trimountain, nach den drei Hügeln, die die Halbinsel beherrschten, Mount Pemberton, Mount Vernon und Beacon Hill. Nur letzterer hat sich erhalten, wenn auch in stark verkleinerter Form, die anderen beiden wurden vollständig abgetragen, mit ihnen füllte man im 19. Jh. die Niederungen und Salzsümpfe längs der Küste auf. Das Gebiet der Halbinsel hat heute die dreifache Oberfläche von 1630 und die Landgewinnung von Boston gilt als eine der größten Ingeneurleistungen der amerikanischen Geschichte.

BOSTON: LES ORIGINES

Des fouilles ont prouvé l'existence au Massachusetts d'implantations humaines remontant à 3000 ans environ. La péninsule sur laquelle devait être bâtie la ville de Boston était jadis habitée par des tribus algonquiennes qui l'appelaient Shawmut ("Là où trouver des bateaux") mais la population indigène fut pratiquement décimée par les maladies introduites par les Européens qui commencèrent à explorer cette partie du littoral atlantique au XVIe siècle.

Les premières installations de colons européens autour de la Massachusetts Bay datent des années 1630, époque à laquelle y arrivèrent les puritains fuyant l'Angleterre et ses persécutions. Un groupe nombreux était conduit par John Winthrop qui, ayant obtenu en 1629 une charte de colonie indépendante de la Couronne britannique,

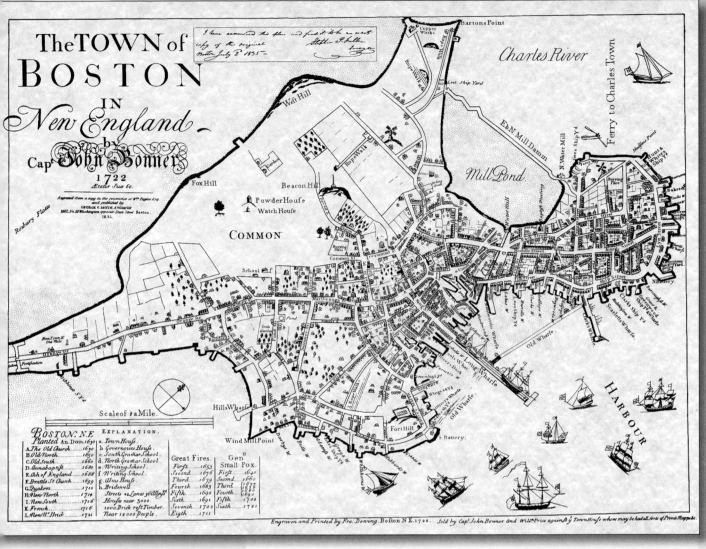

Boston in a map dated 1722.　　　　Carte de Boston datant de 1722.

Boston auf einem Plan von 1722.　　　　1722年の地図の中のボストン

y instaura un gouvernement autonome. Les nouveaux colons appelèrent l'endroit Boston, du nom de la ville natale de nombre d'entre eux, en Angleterre dans le Lincolnshire (ville dont le saint patron était saint Botolph, patron des pêcheurs). Dans un premier temps, la bourgade coloniale s'était toutefois appelée Trimountain ou Tremont, en raison des trois collines qui dominaient la péninsule: Mount Pemberton, Mount Vernon et Beacon Hill. Seule la dernière subsiste, encore que très réduite: les deux autres furent arasées au XIXe siècle et leur terre utilisée pour combler les marécages du bord de mer. La superficie de la péninsule a ainsi triplé depuis 1630 et l'extension de la ville sur les terrains artificiels est l'une des plus grandes réalisations d'ingénierie de l'histoire américaine.

● ボストン：その起源

考古学的遺跡の発掘の結果、3000年前からマサチューセッツには定住民族がいたことが分かった。アルゴンキン系諸部族などのネイティブアメリカンは、現在ボストン市がある半島に住み、この土地を『シャウムツ』（＜ボートが見える場所＞という意味）と呼んだ。定住していたネイティブアメリカンたちは、16世紀に大西洋に面するこの一帯にやって来た最初のヨーロッパ人探検家に移された病気で全滅してしまった。
マサチューセッツ湾一帯に入植した最初のヨーロッパ人は、1630年の英国の迫害を逃れてきた清教徒たちで、特に数が多かったのはジョン・ウィンスロップが率いるグループだった。彼は1629年に英国王チャールズ1世から独立植民特許状を獲得し、自治植民地を建設した人物だ。多くの移民の故郷

であるリンコルシールのボストンに因んで、ここはボストンと名付けられた。元来ボストンという名称は、セント・ボトルフBotolph(古英語でbotは＜ボート＞、ulphは＜助け＞という意味)に由来する。この聖人は漁師とイギリスのボストン市の守護聖人だ。植民地は最初トリマウンテンと名付けられた。半島には、ペンバートン山、ヴァーノン山、ビーコン・ヒルの3つの丘がそびえていたからだ。3つの丘のうち残ったのはビーコン・ヒルだけだが、昔に比べるとかなり小さくなっている。他の2つは平らになり、19世紀には沼地や海岸沿いの湿地帯に変ってしまった。実際に半島の土地は1630年に比べると3倍に広がった。ボストンの領土拡張はアメリカ史上最大の土木工事の一つとして考えられている。

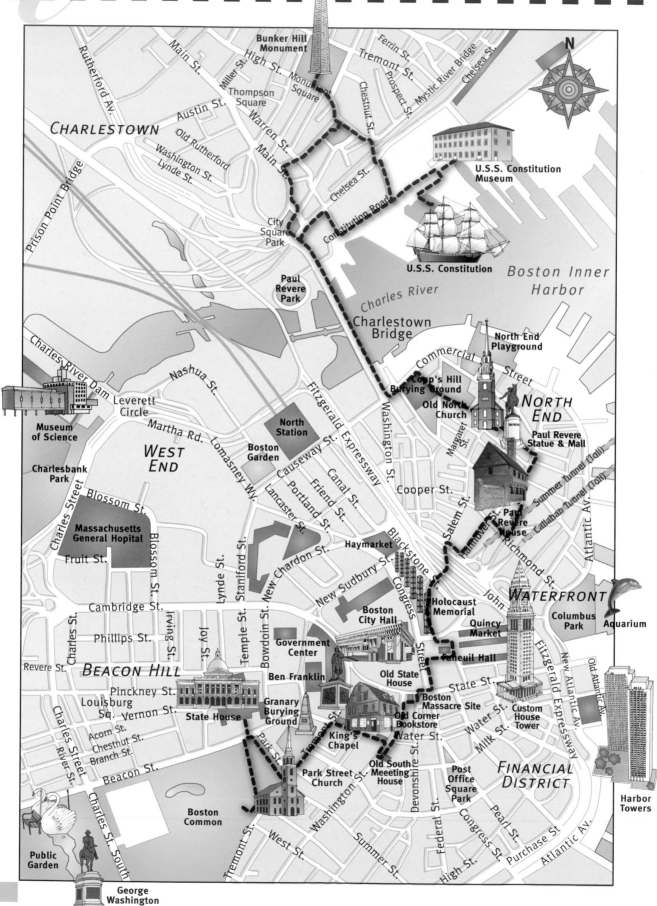

FREEDOM TRAIL

The city of Boston was the theater of many important episodes in the colonies' fight for independence from the British Crown and in American history in general. Everyone remembers the **Boston Tea Party**, when Patriots disguised as Indians threw hundreds of pounds of tea into the bay as a protest against the English government's Tea Tax. The documentation concerning this event is preserved in a museum, which together with many other historical sites in the city goes to make up the **Freedom Trail**, a walking tour of the places that marked America's march toward independence. Running from the present **State House**, the headquarters built for the post-Revolutionary government of the Bay State, to the berth of the **USS Constitution**, the first large vessel of the US Navy, the Freedom Trail permits us to renew and deepen our acquaintance with important historical episodes and figures. We must not forget that many of the patriots and statesmen that made American history were born or lived in Boston. **Benjamin Franklin**, **John Hancock**, **Samuel Adams**, and **Paul Revere** are only a few of the many personalities whose deeds and words accompany us along this fascinating walk through American history.

Die Stadt Boston war Schauplatz vieler bedeutender Ereignisse während des Freiheitskampfes der Kolonien gegen die englische Krone. Jeder weiß von der **Boston Tea Party**, als Patrioten, die sich als Indianer verkleidet hatten, hunderte von Teepaketen in die Bucht warfen, um gegen die von der englischen Regierung auferlegte Teesteuer zu protestieren. Die Dokumentation dazu befindet sich in einem Museum, das zusammen mit anderen historischen Schauplätzen in der Stadt zum **Freedom Trail** (Freiheitspfad) gehört, ein Rundgang, der Amerikas Weg in die Freiheit erläutert. Er führt von dem heutigen **State House**, dem Hauptquartier der nachrevolutionären Regierung des Bay State, bis zum Liegeplatz der **USS Constitution**, dem ersten großen Schiff der US-Kriegsmarine und ermöglicht es, unsere Kenntnisse über wichtige historische Episoden und Persönlichkeiten zu vertiefen. Viele Patrioten und Staatsmänner der amerikanischen Geschichte lebten in Boston oder wurden dort geboren: **Benjamin Franklin**, **John Hancock**, **Samuel Adams** und **Paul Revere** sind nur einige von denen, deren Taten und Worte uns bei diesem faszinierenden Rundgang durch die Geschichte begleiten werden.

La ville de Boston fut le théâtre d'épisodes majeurs de l'histoire américaine, surtout durant la lutte pour l'Indépendance. Le plus connu est indubitablement la révolte dite **"Boston Tea Party"** au cours de laquelle des patriotes jetèrent dans la baie une cargaison de thé pour protester contre les taxes d'importation que leur imposait le gouvernement anglais. La documentation de cet événement est conservée au musée qui, avec de nombreux autres sites et monuments historiques de la ville, forme le **Freedom Trail**. Ce circuit historique pédestre qui illustre la marche de l'Amérique vers l'indépendance va de la **Massachusetts State House**, construite à l'origine pour le gouvernement postrévolutionnaire du Bay State, jusqu'au quai où est amarrée la frégate **USS Constitution**, premier bâtiment de la marine américaine. Une "Voie de la liberté" qui permet de se plonger au cœur de l'histoire américaine et d'en mieux connaître les personnages. Nombre des patriotes et hommes politiques qui ont écrit cette histoire étaient, en effet, originaires de Boston ou y vécurent: **Benjamin Franklin**, **John Hancock**, **Samuel Adams** et **Paul Revere**, entre autres.

フリーダム・トレイル（自由の道）
ボストン市は、イギリスからの独立戦争をはじめアメリカ史全般の数多くの重要事件の舞台となった。**ボストン茶会事件**は誰もが知っているだろう。英国政府が課した茶税に反対して、インディアンに扮した愛国者が何百ポンドもの茶を海に投げ捨てた事件だ。この事件に関する資料が納められている博物館は、市内の多くの史跡とともに**フリーダム・トレイル**を形成している。これは独立へのアメリカの歩みをしるす歴史的遺産を徒歩で巡る観光コースだ。ベイ・ステートの革命後政権のために建設された現在の**州庁舎**から始まるこのツアーでは、米国海軍史上初の大型軍艦**USSコンスティテューション号**の停泊地などを回り、アメリカ史上の重要事件やその立役者になった人物たちに関する知識を新たにし、また一層深めることができる。アメリカの歴史を作った愛国者や政治家の多くはボストン生まれかボストンに住んだという事実を忘れてはならない。**ベンジャミン・フランクリン**、**ジョン・ハンコック**、**サミュエル・アダムス**、**ポール・リヴィア**などの多くの人物の言葉と行動が、アメリカ史をつづるフリーダム・トレイル・ツアーに魅力を与えている。

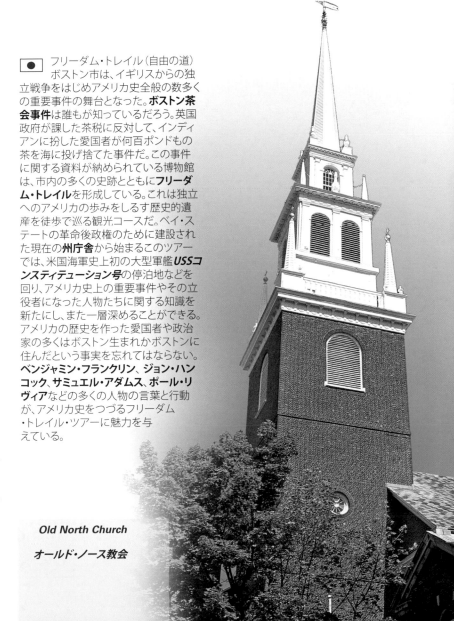

Old North Church

オールド・ノース教会

BOSTON COMMON
& BOSTON PUBLIC GARDEN

Boston Common, purchased by the city in **1634**, embraces a number of sites of historical interest, first and foremost the ***Robert Gould Shaw and 54th Regiment Memorial***. This bronze relief, created by **Augustus Saint-Gaudens** (1897), recalls a battle of the US Civil War, when for the first time blacks officially participated in the military and thus the civil life of the country; the monument is the starting point of the **Black Heritage Trail®**. On the south side of the park is the **Central Burying Ground**, the last resting place of the British soldiers who fell during the Battle of Bunker Hill (1775). The **State House**, seat Massachusetts' state government, faces the northwest side of the park; the magnificent **Park Street Church** instead stands at the corner of Park Street and Tremont Street. Across Charles Street from the Boston Common is the entrance to the **Boston Public Garden**.

Der Park Boston Common wurde **1634** von der Stadt erworben, zu ihm gehören eine Reihe historischer Schauplätze. Das ***Robert Gould Shaw and 54th Regiment Memorial*** ist ein Bronzerelief, das **Augustus Saint-Gaudens** 1897 schuf, es erinnert an eine Schlacht des amerikanischen Bürgerkriegs, als zum ersten Mal offiziell Schwarze in der Armee dienten. Das Denkmal steht am Beginn des **Black Heritage Trail®** (Pfad des Erbes der Schwarzen). An der Südseite des Parks befindet sich der **Central Burying Ground**, hier wurden die englischen Soldaten beigesetzt, die in der Schlacht von Bunker Hill fielen (1775). Im **State House** an der Nordwestseite des Parks hat die Staatsregierung von Massachusetts ihren Sitz. Die prächtige **Park Street Church** steht an der Ecke von Park und Tremont Street. Gegenüber von Boston Common, jenseits der Charles Street, betritt man den **Boston Public Garden.**

"Robert Gould Shaw and 54th Regiment Memorial"

<ロバート・グッド・ショーと第54連隊記念碑>

Public Garden, statue of *George Washington*.

Public Garden, Statue des *George Washington*.

Public Garden, statue de *George Washington*.

パブリック・ガーデン、ジョージ・ワシントン像

Propriété municipale depuis **1634**, le Boston Common est un gigantesque espace vert englobant plusieurs sites et monuments historiques importants, à commencer par le *Robert Gould Shaw and 54th Regiment Memorial.* Ce monument en bronze, dû à **Augustus Saint-Gaudens** (1897), commémore le colonel Shaw et son régiment – première unité de Noirs engagés officiellement dans la guerre de Sécession et donc dans la vie civile du pays – et constitue le point de départ du **Black Heritage Trail®**. Au sud du parc, le **Central Burying Ground** est le cimetière où reposent les soldats Britanniques tombés à la bataille de Bunker Hill (1775). La **Massachusetts State House**, où siège le gouvernement de l'État, se trouve au nord-ouest du parc tandis que la superbe **Park Street Church** se dresse à l'angle de Park St. et de Tremont St. Quant à lui, le jardin public, **Boston Public Garden**, est séparé du Boston Common, qu'il prolonge, par la Charles St.

ボストン・コモンと
ボストン・パブリック・ガーデン
ボストン・コモン：**1634年**ボストン市が購入したこの場所には史跡が多い。まず注目したいのは、*ロバート・グッド・ショーと第54連隊記念碑*だ。**オーガスタス・セント＝ゴーデンス**が製作したブロンズの浅浮き彫りで(1897年)、アメリカ南北戦争が題材だ。これは黒人が公式に参加した最初の戦争で、黒人が公民として最初に参加した国事として考えられる。記念碑は**ブラック・ヘリテージ・トレイル**の出発点だ。公園の南側に広がる**セントラル墓地**には、バンカー・ヒルの戦い(1775年)で亡くなった兵士たちが埋葬されている。公園の北西側に立つ**州庁舎**には、マサチューセッツ州政府が置かれている。美しい**パーク・ストリート教会**はパーク・ストリートとトリモント・ストリートの角に位置する。ボストン・コモンからチャールズ・ストリートを横切ると**ボストン・パブリック・ガーデン**の入口に至る。

CHARLES BULFINCH
(1763-1844)

Charles Bulfinch is considered America's first professional architect and the greatest exponent of the **Federal Style**. After having completed his studies at Harvard College, he traveled extensively in Europe where he came into contact with Italian Classicism and the works of the English architects Christopher Wren and Robert Adam. Upon his return to Boston, Bulfinch elaborated on his European gleanings and so gave rise to the Federal style in architecture, marked by classical composition of volumes and motifs. Bulfinch was largely responsible for transforming the colonial town of Boston into a true American city. Among the many buildings designed by Bulfinch in that period, the most important extant examples are the central portion of the State House and the Harrison Gray Otis House.

Charles Bulfinch gilt als der erste professionell arbeitende Architekt Amerikas und der bedeutendste Vertreter des **Federal Style**. Nach dem Studium am Harvard College unternahm er ausgedehnte Reisen durch Europa, wo er den italienischen Klassizismus untersuchte und die Werke der englischen Architekten Christopher Wren und Robert Adam kennen lernte. Nach seiner Rückkehr verarbeitete Bulfinch in Boston diese Erfahrungen und verwirklichte den Federal Style, den in Volumen und Motiven eine klassische Komposition auszeichnet. Bulfinch war überwiegend dafür verantwortlich, dass die Kolonialstadt Boston in eine wahre amerikanische Stadt verwandelt wurde. Unter den vielen Bauwerken, die er in dieser Zeit entwarf, gibt es noch den zentralen Teil des State House und das Harrison Gray Otis House.

Charles Bulfinch est considéré comme le premier architecte professionnel américain et le chef de file du **Style Fédéral**. Après ses études à Harvard College, il voyagea à travers l'Europe où il entra en contact avec le classicisme italien et les travaux des architectes anglais Christopher Wren et Robert Adam. De retour à Boston, il mit cette "moisson européenne" à profit et donna naissance au style fédéral en architecture, un style marqué par une composition classique des volumes et des motifs. C'est surtout grâce à lui que, de petite ville coloniale, Boston se transforma en véritable cité américaine. Des nombreux édifices qu'il conçut, les plus importants que l'on puisse voir aujourd'hui sont la State House (partie centrale) et la Harrison Gray Otis House.

チャールズ・ブルフィンチ (Charles Bulfinch) はアメリカで最初の専門建築家で、**フェデラル様式**を提唱した人物だ。ハーヴァード大学で学んだ後ヨーロッパを旅行した彼は、イタリア古典主義や英国建築家クリストファー・ウレンやロバート・アダムの作品に触発された。ボストン帰着後、ブルフィンチはヨーロッパで収集した知識を発展させ、古典様式の量感と装飾要素を特徴としたフェデラル様式を確立し、ボストンを一介の植民地からモダンなアメリカ都市に変身させた。この時期にブルフィンチが設計した多数の建造物の中でも特に重要なのは、州庁舎の中心部とハリソン・グレイ・オーティス邸だ。

JFK Statue

ジョン・F.ケネディ像

MASSACHUSETTS STATE HOUSE

The new State House, designed by **Charles Bulfinch**, is considered a masterpiece of American Federal style. A large dome—covered in 23K gold sheet—surmounts the center portion in red brick profiled with refined white moldings. The ground floor foyer is also known as the **Doric Hall**. Upstairs, in the **Hall of Flags**, the flags of all the Massachusetts regiments in service from the Civil War through the Vietnam War are displayed on a rotating basis. The third floor is entirely given over to the grandiose halls of the state legislature: the **House of Representatives** and the **Senate Chamber**. Hanging over the public gallery in the House is the famous *Sacred Cod* symbolizing the importance of the fishing industry in the early Massachusetts economy. A statue honoring Boston-born President **John F. Kennedy** stands in front of the State House.

Das neue State House im amerikanischen Federal Style entwarf **Charles Bulfinch**, es gilt als sein Meisterwerk. Die mit 23-karätigem Blattgold ausgelegte Kuppel bekrönt den zentralen Teil des Bauwerks aus rotem Backstein, mit seinen weißen Gesimsen und Leisten. Die Halle des Erdgeschosses nennt sich **Doric Hall**. Oben, in der **Hall of Flags** versammelte man alle Fahnen der Regimenter Massachusetts', die vom Bürgerkrieg bis zum Vietnam-Krieg in der Armee dienten. Der dritte Stock enthält die Säle der gesetzgebenden Versammlung des Bundesstaates, das **Repräsentantenhaus** und den **Senat**. In der Public Gallery im Repräsentantenhaus findet man den *Sacred Cod* (der heilige Kabeljau), der die Bedeutung des Fischfangs für das frühe Massachusetts symbolisiert. Vor dem Haus steht eine Statue des in Boston geborenen Präsidenten **John F. Kennedy**.

La nouvelle State House, siège du gouvernement du Massachusetts, fut construite par **Charles Bulfinch**. C'est un chef-d'œuvre du style fédéral américain avec son grand dôme – revêtu d'or à 23 carats – coiffant la partie centrale de l'édifice en brique rouge que soulignent de beaux éléments de couleur blanche. Au rez-de-chaussée, se trouve le foyer appelé **Doric Hall** et, au premier l'étage, le **Hall of Flags** où, sur une plateforme tournante, sont présentés les drapeaux de tous les régiments du Massachusetts ayant servi leur pays, de la guerre de Sécession jusqu'à la guerre du Vietnam. Le troisième étage est entièrement occupé par les salles grandioses du gouvernement: la **Senate Chamber** et la **House of Representatives** (salle des Représentants). La morue séchée, appelée *Sacred Cod*, qui est suspendue au-dessus de la galerie du public est le symbole d'une des principales sources de revenus du Massachusetts à ses débuts. En face de la State House, statue du président **John F. Kennedy**, natif de Boston.

マサチューセッツ州庁舎
チャールズ・ブルフィンチが設計した新州庁舎はアメリカ・フェデラル様式の傑作といわれている。23カラットの金箔で覆われた巨大なドームが、白い刳形で輪郭を描いた赤レンガの建物中央部を覆っている。一階のロビーは**ドーリック・ホール**とも呼ばれる。二階の**フラッグ・ホール**には、南北戦争からヴェトナム戦争まで戦争に参加したマサチューセッツ連隊の旗が総て回転台の上に飾られている。三階は**下院**と**上院**が置かれた州立法府だ。州庁舎内のギャラリーを飾るのは**聖なるタラ**で、植民当初マサチューセッツでは漁業が主要産業だったことを象徴している。州庁舎の前には、ボストン生まれの合衆国大統領**ジョン・F.ケネディ**像が立つ。

Interiors.
Innenansicht.
Intérieur.
内部

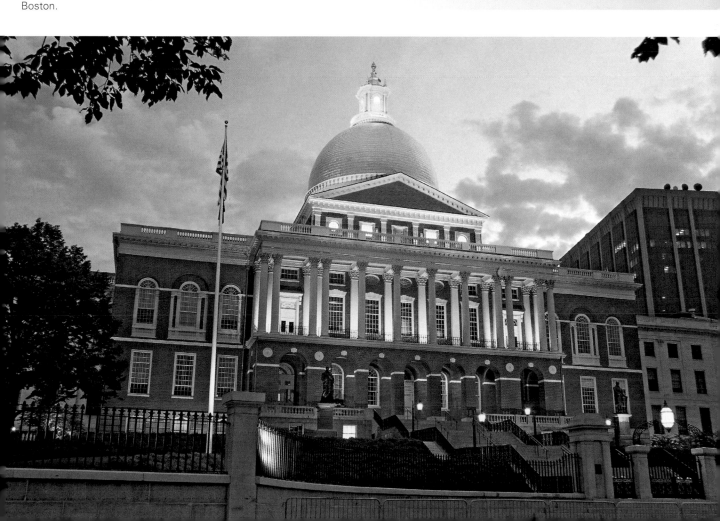

PARK STREET CHURCH

This church, inaugurated in 1809, is one of the finest examples of religious architecture in Boston. The architect was Peter Banner, who took his inspiration from **St. Bride's Church** in London. Architectural qualities aside, Park Street Church is famous principally for the activities and the events that took place there. Since the very beginning of its history, the church was a center of humanitarian initiatives: in 1810 it became the headquarters of the **Committee for American Missions Abroad**; in 1824 it was the meeting place of the **Prison Reform Society**; it was here that **William Lloyd Garrison** delivered his first Abolitionist speech in 1829. But the most important symbolic event in the history of this church is without a doubt the first public singing of the patriotic song **"America!"** on the Fourth of July 1831. The corner of Tremont and Park Streets on which the church stands is ill-famed as **"Brimstone Corner."** The name, which in the past was assigned to the church as well as its location, probably derives from the fact that the crypt served as a storehouse for the sulfur used to prepare gunpowder during the War of 1812; other sources, instead, attribute the origin of the appellation to the ardent sermons delivered from the church's pulpit. Although Park Street Church is now surrounded by much taller buildings, its bell tower continues to dominate Boston Common with extraordinary grace.

Diese 1809 geweihte Kirche ist eines der schönsten Beispiele religiöser Architektur in Boston. Der Architekt hieß Peter Banner, er inspirierte sich an der **St. Bride's Church** in London. Von der Architektur einmal abgesehen ist die Park Street Church vor allem wegen der Ereignisse und Initiativen berühmt, die mit ihr verbunden sind. Schon 1810 befand sich hier das Hauptquartier des **Komitees für Amerikanische Missionen im Ausland**, 1824 war sie der Treffpunkt für die **Gesellschaft der Gefängnisreform** und **William Lloyd Garrison** hielt hier 1829 seine erste Rede zur Abschaffung der Sklaverei. Hier wurde am 4. Juli 1831 zum ersten Mal das patriotische Lied **„Amerika!"** angestimmt, wohl das symbolisch bedeutendste Ereignis in der Kirchengeschichte. Die Ecke zwischen Tremont und Park Street, wo die Kirche steht, hat den anrüchigen Namen **„Brimstone Corner"** (Schwefelsteinecke). Früher belegte man nicht nur den Ort, sondern auch die Kirche mit dieser Bezeichnung, wahrscheinlich weil die Krypta als Lager für den Schwefel diente, den man während des Krieges von 1812 für die Zubereitung von Schießpulver verwandte. Andere Quellen bringen dies jedoch eher mit den flammenden Predigten in Zusammenhang, die hier von der Kanzel zu hören waren. Obwohl die Kirche inzwischen von wesentlich höheren Bauwerken umgeben ist, dominiert in Boston Common immer noch ihr eleganter Glockenturm.

Cette église, inaugurée en 1809, est un des plus beaux exemples de l'architecture religieuse de Boston. Son architecte, Peter Banner, s'inspira de **St Bride's Church** à Londres. Outre ses qualités architecturales, l'église est célèbre pour les activités et les événements dont elle fut le théâtre. Dès le tout début de son histoire, elle fut au centre des initiatives humanitaires: siège du **Comité pour les missions américaines à l'étranger** en 1810, elle servit de lieu de réunion à la **Société pour la réforme des prisons** en 1824. C'est aussi ici qu'en 1829 **William Lloyd Garrison** prononça son premier discours abolitionniste. Toutefois, l'événement le plus important et le plus symbolique reste indubitablement le fait qu'on y ait chanté pour la première fois l'hymne patriotique **"America!"**, le 4 juillet 1831. L'angle de Tremont St. et de Park St. où se dresse l'église est appelé **"Brimstone Corner"**. Ce surnom qui, jadis désignait aussi bien l'église que ses environs, vient probablement du fait que sa crypte servit pendant la guerre de 1812 de dépôt de souffre (*brimstone*) dont on faisait la poudre à fusil; d'autres sources, l'attribuent aux sermons enflammés prononcés du haut de sa chaire. Bien que Park Street Church soit désormais entourée de gratte-ciel, son clocher continue de dominer le Boston Common avec une grâce extraordinaire.

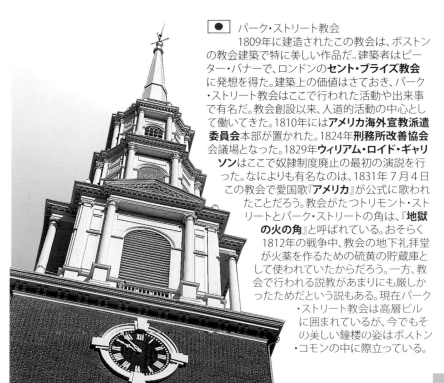

パーク・ストリート教会
　1809年に建造されたこの教会は、ボストンの教会建築で特に美しい作品だ。建築者はピーター・バナーで、ロンドンの**セント・ブライズ教会**に発想を得た。建築上の価値はさておき、パーク・ストリート教会はここで行われた活動や出来事で有名だ。教会創設以来、人道的活動の中心として働いてきた。1810年には**アメリカ海外宣教派遣委員会**本部が置かれた。1824年**刑務所改善協会**会議場となった。1829年**ウィリアム・ロイド・ギャリソン**はここで奴隷制度廃止の最初の演説を行った。なによりも有名なのは、1831年7月4日この教会で愛国歌**『アメリカ』**が公式に歌われたことだろう。教会がたつトリモント・ストリートとパーク・ストリートの角は、『**地獄の火の角**』と呼ばれている。おそらく1812年の戦争中、教会の地下礼拝堂が火薬を作るための硫黄の貯蔵庫として使われていたからだろう。一方、教会で行われる説教があまりにも厳しかったためだという説もある。現在パーク・ストリート教会は高層ビルに囲まれているが、今でもその美しい鐘楼の姿はボストン・コモンの中に際立っている。

GRANARY BURYING GROUND

Boston's cemeteries number among the most historically significant in all the United States, and among them, the Granary Burying Ground is certainly the most celebrated. The gravestones and richly-decorated obelisks mark the burial places of such historical figures as **Samuel Adams**, **John Hancock**, and **Paul Revere**.

Die Friedhöfe Bostons zählen zu den historisch bedeutendsten der gesamten Vereinigten Staaten und der berühmteste ist sicherlich der Granary Burying Ground. Die Grabsteine und reich dekorierten Obeliske stehen an den Gräbern herausragender Persönlichkeiten wie **Samuel Adams**, **John Hancock** und **Paul Revere**.

Boston possède plusieurs cimetières historiques parmi les plus importants des États-Unis, dont le Granary Burying Ground est certainement l'un des plus célèbres. Obélisques et pierres tombales aux riches ornements indiquent ici la sépulture de personnages historiques illustres tels que **Samuel Adams**, **John Hancock** et **Paul Revere**.

グラナリー墓地
ボストン市内の墓地は全米で最も重要な史跡に数えられる。その中でグラナリー墓地は特に有名だ。豊かな装飾が施された墓石や方尖塔は、**サミュエル・アダムス**、**ジョン・ハンコック**、**ポール・リヴィア**などの歴史的に重要な人物が埋葬された場所を示している。

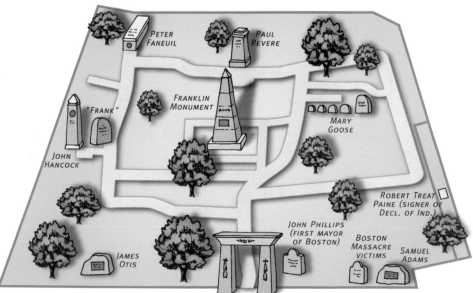

Tremont Street

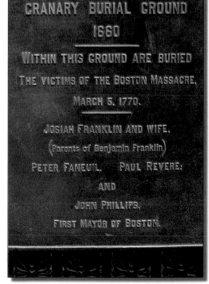

KING'S CHAPEL

🇺🇸 Ordered built by Royal Governor **Sir Edmund Andros** in 1686 as a place of worship for those of the Anglican faith, this church immediately aroused the intense opposition of Puritan Bostonians. The first church was in wood, as were all the early Colonial buildings, but in 1749 the architect **Peter Harrison** was charged with styling a project for expansion. The new King's Chapel is in Georgian style with walls of Quincy granite. Unfortunately, money ran out before the bell tower could be completed—and it is still unfinished. King's Chapel was considered a symbol of English tyranny and was closed after the colonies had achieved independence. In 1782, it was reopened as the first **Unitarian Church** in the US. Its bell, installed in 1816, was cast by Paul Revere's shop; Revere defined it as "my sweetest sounding bell." Outside, on the north side, is Boston's first cemetery, the **King's Chapel Burying Ground**. Among its "guests" are **John Winthrop**, a city founder and the first Governor of the Boston colony, **Mary Chilton Winslow**, the first English woman to set foot on the soil of the New World as she disembarked from the *Mayflower* at Plymouth in 1620, and **Samuel Prescott** and **William Dawes Jr.**, protagonists, together with Paul Revere, of the famous "midnight ride."

🇩🇪 Die Kapelle ließ der königliche Gouverneur **Sir Edmund Andros** 1686 als Andachtsraum für die Anglikaner errichten, nicht ohne die Opposition der Puritaner Bostons zu provozieren. Wie alle Gebäude der Kolonialzeit war sie aus Holz, aber 1749 beauftragte man den Architekten **Peter Harrison** mit dem Erweiterungsbau und die neue Kapelle im Georgian Style erhielt Mauern aus Quincy-Granit. Vor Beendigung des Glockenturms ging das Geld aus und er blieb unvollendet. Die King's Chapel galt als ein Symbol der englischen Tyrannis und man schloss sie nach der Unabhängigkeit der Kolonien. Erst 1782 konnte sie als die erste **Unitarian Church** der USA wiedereröffnet werden. Die 1816 aufgehängte Glocke wurde in der Werkstatt von Paul Revere gegossen, der sie als seine am süßesten klingende Glocke bezeichnete. An der Nordseite der Kirche erstreckt sich Bostons erster Friedhof, der **King's Chapel Burying Ground**, dort liegen **John Winthrop**, einer der Stadtgründer und der erste Gouverneur der Kolonie Boston, dann **Mary Chilton Winslow**, die erste Engländerin, die ihren Fuß auf die Neue Welt setzte, als sie 1620 in Plymouth die *Mayflower* verließ und außerdem **Samuel Prescott** und **William Dawes Jr.**, die zusammen mit Paul Revere den berühmten „midnight ride" durchführten.

🇫🇷 Bâtie en 1686 à la demande du gouverneur royal **Sir Edmund Andros** comme lieu de prière pour les anglicans, cette église déchaîna immédiatement l'opposition des puritains de Boston. L'église originelle était en bois, comme tous les bâtiments coloniaux, mais en 1749 l'architecte **Peter Harrison** fut chargé de l'agrandir. La nouvelle King's Chapel fut construite en granite de Quincy dans le style géorgien. Toutefois, faute de moyens, son clocher ne fut jamais terminé et est encore inachevé. Considérée comme un symbole de la tyrannie anglaise, King's Chapel fut fermée après l'Indépendance mais, rouverte en 1782, elle devint la première **église unitarienne** des États-Unis. Sa cloche, installée en 1816, fut fabriquée dans la fonderie de Paul Revere qui l'appelait "Ma cloche la plus douce". À l'extérieur, côté nord, se trouve le tout premier cimetière de Boston: **King's Chapel Burying Ground** où reposent entre autres **John Winthrop**, l'un des fondateurs de Boston et son premier gouverneur, **Mary Chilton Winslow**, la première Anglaise à avoir foulé le sol du Nouveau Monde en débarquant du *Mayflower* à Plymouth en 1620, ainsi que **Samuel Prescott** et **William Dawes Jr.** qui, avec Paul Revere, furent les protagonistes de la fameuse "Chevauchée nocturne".

🇯🇵 キングス・チャペル
　英国王から派遣された総督**エドモン・アンドロス卿**が1686年に英国国教会として建築を命じたこの建物は、ただちにボストンの清教徒たちの激しい反抗を受けた。当時の他の建築物と同様、最初の教会は木造だったが、1749年建築家**ピーター・ハリソン**に拡張計画が依頼された。新しいキングス・チャペルは外壁にクインシー産大理石を使ったジョージ朝様式の建物だ。残念ながら鐘楼が完成する前に建築資金が底をついたため、鐘楼は未完のままだ。キングス・チャペルは英国の圧政の象徴として考えられたため、植民地が独立を勝ち取った後は閉鎖された。その後1782年にアメリカ初の**ユニタリアン教会**となった。1816年に設置されたこの教会の鐘は、ポール・リヴィアの工房で鋳造されたものだ。リヴィアは「私の優しい鐘の音」と呼んだ。教会の北側に広がる**キングス・チャペル墓地**は、ボストン最初の墓地だ。ここに埋葬されている人々の中には、町の創設者でボストン植民地初代総督**ジョン・ウィンスロップ**、1620年メイフラワー号でプリマスに到着し、新世界に足を踏み入れた初のイギリス人女性**メアリー・チルトン・ウィンスロウ**、また『ミッドナイト・ライド』でポール・リヴィアと一緒に活躍した**プリスコット**や**ウィリアム・ドウズJr**などの墓もある。

BOSTON LATIN SCHOOL
& BENJAMIN FRANKLIN STATUE

Another of Boston's many "firsts" is the founding of the first public secondary school in the United States (the Boston Latin School) in 1635. The original building was demolished in 1749 to make room for enlarging King's Chapel. The statues of **Benjamin Franklin** and Mayor **Joshua Quincy** now mark the site of the school these illustrious students once attended.

Ein weiteres der vielen Primate Bostons ist 1635 die Gründung der ersten höheren Schule in den Staaten, nämlich der Boston Latin School. Das ursprüngliche Gebäude wurde 1749 für die Erweiterung der King's Chapel abgerissen. Die Statuen von **Benjamin Franklin** und Bürgermeister **Joshua Quincy** stehen jetzt an derselben Stelle, wo sie einst zur Schule gingen.

Parmi les nombreuses primautés de Boston figure la fondation, en 1635, de la première école publique des États-Unis, la Boston Latin School dont l'ancien bâtiment fut démoli en 1749 lors des travaux d'agrandissement de la King's Chapel. Aujourd'hui, les statues du président **Benjamin Franklin** et de **Joshua Quincy**, maire de Boston, indiquent l'emplacement de l'école dont ils furent les illustres élèves.

ボストン・ラテン・スクールとベンジャミン・フランクリン像
ボストンでは「全米初の出来事」がたくさんあるが、その一つとして挙げられるのは、1635年に合衆国初の中等学校(ボストン・ラテン・スクール)が設立されたことだ。残念ながらキングス・チャペルの拡張工事で、1749年にオリジナルの建物は破壊された。この学校の生徒だった**ベンジャミン・フランクリン**像と市長**ジョシュア・クインシー**像がその跡地にたっている。

OLD CORNER BOOKSTORE

This ancient bookstore, at the corner of School and Washington Street, is part of Boston's history. The building originally belonged to the apothecary Thomas Crease; it then passed from hand to hand until the publisher **William Ticknor** purchased it in 1833. Just a few years later, **Ticknor & Fields** was one of the most important publishing houses in the US and its premises a favorite meeting place for American and foreign people of letters: **Ralph Waldo Emerson**, **Henry David Thoreau**, **Louise May Alcott**, **Harriet Beecher Stowe**, and **Nathaniel Hawthorne**, to cite only a few.

Cette ancienne librairie, située à l'angle de School St. et de Washington St., fait partie intégrante de l'histoire de Boston. Le bâtiment, qui à l'origine avait appartenu à un apothicaire, Thomas Crease, changea plusieurs fois de propriétaire avant d'être acheté par l'éditeur **William Ticknor** en 1833. Quelques année plus tard, la maison d'édition **Ticknor & Fields** était devenue l'une des plus importantes des États-Unis et son siège, un lieu de rencontre littéraire fréquenté par d'innombrables écrivains américains et étrangers, dont **Ralph Waldo Emerson**, **Henry David Thoreau**, **Louise May Alcott**, **Harriet Beecher Stowe** et **Nathaniel Hawthorne**.

Dieser alte Buchladen an der Ecke School und Washington Street ist ebenfalls Teil der Geschichte Bostons. Der Bau gehörte ursprünglich dem Apotheker Thomas Crease, wechselte dann mehrfach den Besitzer und wurde schließlich von dem Verleger William Ticknor erworben (1833). Wenige Jahre später galt Ticknor & Fields als einer der bedeutendsten Verlage Amerikas und dort stellten sich folglich amerikanische und ausländische Schriftsteller ein, **Ralph Waldo Emerson**, **Henry David Thoreau**, **Louise May Alcott**, **Harriett Beecher Stowe** und **Nathaniel Hawthorne**, um nur einige zu nennen.

オールド・コーナー・ブックストア
ラテン・スクールとワシントン・ストリートの角にたつこの古い書店は、ボストン史の一部といえる。オリジナルの建物は薬剤師トーマス・クリースが所有していた。その後何度も所有者が変り、結局1833年に出版者**ウィリアム・ティクナー**が購入した。その後まもなく**ティクナー＆フィールズ**は全米最大の出版社に発展し、この書店はアメリカ内外の数多くの文人たちが集まる場所となった。**ラルフ・ヴァルド・エマーソン、ヘンリー・デヴィッド・ソロー、ルイーズ・メイ・オルコット、ハリエット・ビーチャー・ストウ、ナサニエル・ホーソン**などは、ほんの一例だ。

OLD SOUTH MEETING HOUSE

The Old South Meeting House, which began its rich history in 1669 as a place of prayer and meeting for the **Congregational Church**, is located at the corner of Washington and Milk Streets. **Benjamin Franklin** was baptized here in 1706. Nevertheless, the Old South Meeting House's major claim to fame is undoubtedly the fervent assemblies held here at the time of the **Boston Tea Party**. On the evening of 16 December 1773, more than 5000 citizens of Boston and environs met to decide a course of action regarding the tea-laden ships of the British East India Company anchored in the port. When the impossibility of reaching a compromise with the Royal Governor on the question of abolition of the Tea Tax became patently apparent, the crowd poured out into the streets, and to the cry of "Boston Harbor a teapot tonight" and "Rally Mohawks, bring out your axes, And tell King George we'll pay no taxes" accompanied Patriots disguised as Indians to the port, where history's greatest Tea Party was held that very night.

Das Old South Meeting war ab 1669 das Gebets- und Gemeindehaus der **Congretional Church**. Es liegt an der Ecke zwischen Washington und Milk Street, **Benjamin Franklin** wurde hier 1706 getauft und hier fanden die leidenschaftlichen Versammlungen zur Zeit der **Boston Tea Party** statt. Am Abend des 16. Dezembers 1773 trafen sich mehr als 5000 Bürger aus Boston und Umgebung, um zu entscheiden, was mit den Teeschiffen der Ostindienkompanie geschehen sollte, die im Hafen vor Anker lagen. Als wegen der Abschaffung der Teesteuer kein Kompromiss mit dem königlichen Gouverneur abzusehen war, stürzte die Menge hinaus und unter den Rufen „Boston Harbour a teapot tonight" (Bostons Hafen heute Nacht eine Teekanne) und „Rally Mohawks, bring out your axes and tell King George we'll pay no taxes" (Versammelt Euch Mohikaner, bringt Eure Äxte und sagt König George, dass wir keine Steuern zahlen) begleiteten sie als Indianer verkleidete Patrioten zum Hafen, wo an jenem Abend die größte *Tea Party* der Geschichte stattfand.

Située à l'angle de Washington St. et de Milk St., Old South Meeting House entama sa longue et riche histoire en 1669 comme lieu de prière et de réunion de l'**Église congrégationiste** – c'est ici que **Benjamin Franklin** reçut le baptême en 1706. Mais elle est surtout célèbre pour les assemblées ardentes qui s'y tinrent au moment de la **Boston Tea Party**. Dans la soirée du 16 décembre 1773, plus de 5000 habitants de Boston et des environs s'y réunirent, exaspérés par la présence dans leur port de vaisseaux de la Compagnie des Indes Orientales chargés de thé. L'échec des pourparlers avec le gouverneur royal sur la question de l'abolition de la *Tea Tax*, poussa la foule dans la rue. Criant qu'ils transformeraient leur port en gigantesque théière et appelant la population à se joindre aux Mohawks, les Bostoniens accompagnèrent les patriotes déguisés en Indiens jusqu'aux bateaux dont ils jetèrent la cargaison de thé à la mer. Ce fut la plus grande *Tea Party* de l'histoire!

オールド・サウス集会場
　　オールド・サウス集会場は、1669年**コングリゲーショナル教会**の礼拝と集会の場所として誕生した。ワシントン・ストリートとミルク・ストリートの角に位置する。この教会で1706年に**ベンジャミン・フランクリン**が洗礼を受けた。しかしなんといってもオールド・サウス集会場が有名な理由は、**ボストン茶会事件**前後ここで熱狂的な集会が行われていたからだ。1773年12月16日、ボストンとその周辺から集

まった5,000人余りの住民は、港に碇泊していた英国の東インド会社船の茶陸揚げに対して、どのような行動をとるかを決定した。茶条例廃止問題に関して、英国から派遣された総督と合意は不可能ということがはっきりしたため、通りに殺到した群集は「ボストン湾は今夜ティーポットに」や「モホークよ、集まれ。斧を取り出せ。そしてジョージ王に俺たちは税金を払わないと告げよ。」と叫んで、インディアンに扮した愛国者たちと一緒に港に向かった。その夜、史上名高いボストン茶会事件が起こったのだ。

OLD STATE HOUSE

The Old State House, once known as the **Town House**, is the oldest public building in Boston: in 1711, the original two-story cedar building was rebuilt as we see it today after a serious fire. Like all the public buildings of the time, it served a dual function: civil, as the seat of the administration of the colony, and commercial, as the trade center of the Port of Boston. As British government headquarters, the Old State House was often at the center of protest demonstrations by the colonists; in fact, the tragic massacre of 5 March 1770 was committed right in front of its doors. Later, in 1780, **John Hancock** stood on the same balcony as the first Governor of Massachusetts, but by 1798 the public offices of the state government had already abandoned what had been the symbol of British tyranny and moved to the New State House on Beacon Hill.

Das Old State House, früher auch als **Town House** bekannt, ist das älteste öffentliche Bauwerk Bostons. Im Jahr 1711 wurde das ursprünglich zweistöckige Haus aus Zedernholz nach einem Brand in der heutigen Form erneuert. Wie alle offiziellen Bauten jener Zeit diente es zwei Aufgaben, es war der Verwaltungssitz der Kolonie, aber auch das Handelszentrum des Hafens von Boston. Als Hauptquartier der britischen Verwaltung stand es oftmals im Brennpunkt von Protesten der Kolonisten. Das tragische Massaker vom 5. März 1770 fand direkt vor seinen Toren statt und 1780 stand **John Hancock** auf demselben Balkon, auf dem auch der erste Gouverneur von Massachusetts erschienen war. Doch bereits gegen 1798 verlegte die Staatsregierung die öffentlichen Ämter aus diesem Symbol der englischen Tyrannei in das New State House auf dem Beacon Hill.

L'ancienne State House, qui fut jadis la **Town House**, est le plus vieil édifice public de Boston. Le bâtiment originel, de deux étages en bois de cèdre, fut reconstruit tel que nous le voyons en 1711, après un grave incendie. Comme tous les bâtiments publics de l'époque, il avait une double fonction, servant à la fois de siège à l'administration de la colonie et de centre de négoce du port de Boston. En tant que siège de l'autorité britannique, l'Old State House fut souvent le but des manifestations de protestation des colons. Le massacre perpétré par les Britanniques le 5 mars 1770 eut d'ailleurs lieu sous ses fenêtres. En 1780, c'est du haut de son balcon que **John Hancock**, premier gouverneur du Massachusetts, salua la foule. En 1798, les bureaux publics du gouvernement de l'État avaient déjà quitté ce symbole de la tyrannie britannique pour s'installer dans la New State House, à Beacon Hill.

🔴 旧州庁舎

旧州庁舎は一時**市庁舎**だった建物で、ボストン最古の公共建造物だ。1711年に創建された建物はヒマラヤスギを使った2階建てだったが、大火災の後に現在の姿に建て直された。当時の他の公共建造物と同様、植民地行政府とボストン港交易センターという、二重の役割を果たしていた。英国植民地政府の本拠地が置かれた旧州庁舎は、しばしば植民地住民が反英国運動の抵抗を示した場所でもある。実際、1770年3月5日この建物の前でボストン虐殺事件が起こった。その後1780年、**ジョン・ハンコック**はマサチューセッツ初代州知事としてこの建物のバルコニーに立った。1798年に州政府機関は英国の圧政の象徴だったこの建物から完全に立ち退き、ビーコン・ヒルの新州庁舎に移った。

The **Boston Massacre**, shown here in a famous illustration by Paul Revere's shop, was a bloody step on the Colonies' road to independence from Great Britain. Preceding pages, the facade of the **Old State House**: the unicorn and the lion symbolize the power of the British Empire.

Das **Massaker von Boston**, eine blutige Episode auf dem Weg zur Unabhängigkeit, ist hier auf einer berühmten Illustration aus der Werkstatt von Paul Revere zu sehen. Auf Seite 20-21, die Fassade des **Old State House**; das Einhorn und der Löwe sind die Symbole des Britischen Reichs.

Le **Massacre de Boston**, ici dans une illustration célèbre de l'atelier de Paul Revere, fut une étape sanglante sur la route de l'indépendance des colonies britanniques. Pages 20-21: la façade de l'**Old State House**: la licorne et le lion symbolisent la puissance de l'Empire britannique.

ポール・リヴィアの店に飾られた有名な絵**ボストン虐殺事件**。これは植民地が英国からの独立を目指して辿った長い道のりの中で起こった血生臭い事件だ。前ページの**旧州庁舎**のファサードには英国の権力を象徴する一角獣とライオンが彫られている。

THE BOSTON MASSACRE

The colonial protest and noncompliance aroused by the promulgation of the **Townshend Acts** of 1767 convinced the British Ministry of Defense to garrison about 4000 soldiers in Boston. The Bostonians were not long in demonstrating their antagonism. On the evening of **5 March 1770**, one of these protests turned into tragedy, when a squad of British soldiers shot into the crowd that had been attracted by a fight between a young colonist and a sentinel. Three days later, the entire city came out for the funerals of the victims, who were buried in a common grave in the **Old Granary Burying Ground**.

DAS MASSAKER VON BOSTON

Der Protest der Kolonisten und die Zuwiderhandlungen gegen die **Townshend Acts** von 1767 überzeugten das britischen Verteidigungsministerium davon, in Boston eine Garnison mit 4000 Soldaten einzurichten. Die Einwohner Bostons reagierten und am Abend des **5. März 1770** verwandelte sich eine Protestaktion in Tragödie, als eine Gruppe von britischen Soldaten in die Menge schoss, die sich um einen mit einer Wache kämpfenden jungen Kolonisten geschart hatte. Drei Tage später erschien die gesamte Stadt zum Begräbnis der Opfer, die in einem Massengrab des **Old Granary Burying Ground** beigesetzt wurden.

🇫🇷 LE MASSACRE DE BOSTON

Face à la rébellion des colons qui s'opposaient farouchement aux **Townshed Acts** promulgués en 1767, le ministère de la défense britannique décida d'envoyer 4000 soldats en garnison à Boston. Ce ne fut guère du goût des Bostoniens qui le firent savoir. Le **5 mars 1770**, la énième manifestation tourna au drame lorsque les Anglais tirèrent sur la foule ameutée par un accrochage entre un jeune colon et une sentinelle. Trois jours plus tard, la ville toute entière participa aux obsèques des victimes qui furent enterrées dans une tombe commune à l'**Old Granary Burying Ground**.

 ボストン虐殺事件

1767年に**タウンゼンド条例**が発布された結果、植民地の反発や不従順は増加する一方だった。そこで英国防衛庁は兵士4.000名で構成された駐屯隊をボストンに派遣することを決定した。ボストン市民は直ちに抵抗を示した。**1770年3月5日**の夜、若い入植者と一人の歩哨の間にいさかいが起こった。それに気をとられていた群集に英国軍が発砲したため、一つの抵抗運動が悲劇に変ってしまったのだ。3日後町中の住民が犠牲者の葬儀に参列した。この事件の犠牲者は**旧グラナリー墓地**の共同墓地に埋葬された。

JOHN HANCOCK (1737-1793)

The patriot and statesman John Hancock was the first signer of the Declaration of Independence of 1776. Born into a family of rich Bostonian merchants, he attended Harvard College (now Harvard University) and then entered the business of his uncle Thomas Hancock, from whom he inherited in 1764. Four years later, his self-defense against the accusation of smuggling made him a public figure and a point of reference for the city's Patriots. He was the first Governor of the Commonwealth of Massachusetts, from 1780 to 1785, and held the post again from 1789 until his death.

Der Patriot und Staatsmann John Hancock unterzeichnete 1776 als erster die Unabhängigkeitserklärung. Er stammte aus einer Bostoner Familie reicher Kaufleute, besuchte das Harvard College (heute Harvard University) und trat dann in das Geschäft seines Onkels Thomas Hancock ein, den er 1764 beerbte. Vier Jahre später verteidigte er sich derartig überzeugend gegen eine Schmuggelei-Anklage, dass er zu einer Schlüsselfigur für die Patrioten wurde. Als erster Gouverneur des Commonwealth of Massachusetts amtierte er von 1780 bis 1785 und dann nochmals von 1789 bis zu seinem Tode.

Patriote et homme d'État, John Hancock fut le premier signataire de la Déclaration d'Indépendance en 1776. Issu d'une famille de riches commerçants bostoniens, Hancock fit ses études à Harvard College (actuelle Harvard University) puis intégra l'entreprise de son oncle Thomas Hancock dont il hérita en 1764. Quatre ans plus tard, il se fit connaître en se défendant par lui-même d'une accusation de contrebande et devint une référence pour les patriotes de la ville. John Hancock fut le premier gouverneur du Massachusetts, de 1780 à 1785, puis à nouveau de 1789 jusqu'à sa mort.

ジョン・ハンコック (1737-1793年)

愛国者で政治家でもあるジョン・ハンコックは1776年の独立宣言に最初に署名した人物だ。ボストンの裕福な商家に生まれた彼はハーヴァード・カレッジ(現在のハーヴァード大学)に通った後、伯父トーマス・ハンコックの事業を手伝うようにり、1764年に伯父から遺産を受け継いだ。その4年後密輸罪で告訴された彼は、それに対して自己弁護を始めた。その弁舌によって町の愛国者の中心人物と見なされるようになった。1780年から1785年まで初代マサチューセッツ州知事を務めた。その後1789年から亡くなるまで再度州知事を務めた。

SAMUEL ADAMS (1722-1803)

Patriot and revolutionary, Adams was Boston's most important figure as regards organization of the revolutionary forces before the actual outbreak of war. He was the founder of the city's chapter of the Sons of Liberty, and led the protests that culminated in the Boston Massacre and the Boston Tea Party. As a member of the Second Continental Congress, he was a signer of the Declaration of Independence (1776), the "birth certificate" of the United States of America, but during the war his political standing slipped due to his opposition to the majority plan for establishing a centralized government for the new country. Adams was Lieutenant Governor of Massachusetts from 1789 to 1793 and Governor from 1794 to 1797.

Der Patriot und Revolutionär Adams war in Boston ein Hauptorganisator der revolutionären Truppen, noch ehe der Krieg ausbrach. Er gründete in der Stadt eine Gruppierung der Sons of Liberty (Söhne der Freiheit) und leitete die Protestbewegung, die ihre Höhepunkte im Massaker von Boston und der Boston Tea Party fanden. Als Mitglied des Second Continental Congress unterzeichnete er die Unabhängigkeitserklärung (1776), die „Geburtsurkunde" der Vereinigten Staaten, aber während des Krieges verlor seine politische Position an Boden, denn er stemmte sich gegen den mehrheitlichen Plan einer Zentralregierung für die neue Nation. Adams war Vizegouverneur von Massachusetts (1789-93) und dann Gouverneur (1794-97).

Révolutionnaire et patriote, Samuel Adams fut le personnage central de l'organisation des forces révolutionnaires à Boston avant que n'explose la guerre. Il fut aussi le fondateur du groupe des "Fils de la Liberté" (Sons of Liberty) et le meneur de la protestation qui culmina avec le massacre de Boston et la "Boston Tea Party". Adams participa au Deuxième Congrès Continental (1776), véritable acte de naissance des États-Unis d'Amérique, mais perdit de son prestige politique pendant la guerre lorsqu'il s'opposa au choix, majoritairement défendu, d'instaurer un gouvernement central pour la nouvelle nation. Samuel Adams fut lieutenant-gouverneur du Massachusetts, de 1789 à 1793, puis gouverneur, de 1794 à 1797.

サミュエル・アダムス (1722-1803年)

愛国者であり革命家であるアダムスは、独立戦争勃発前の革命運動家として重要な人物だ。彼は急進結社「自由の息子たち」を結成し、ボストン虐殺事件やボストン茶会事件などの一連の対英ボイコット運動を指導した。また第2回大陸会議に参加して、アメリカ合衆国の誕生を告げる独立宣言書に調印した(1776年)。しかし独立戦争中、政治の中央集権化を目指す多数派と対立したため、彼の政治的地位は低下した。1789年から1793年までマサチューセッツ州副知事、1794年から1797年まで同州知事を務めた。

*The Faneuil Hall's **Assembly Hall**, in **Federal Style**.*

*Die **Assembly Hall** der Faneuil Hall, im **Federal Style** errichtet.*

*L'**Assembly Hall** de Faneuil Hall, de **Style Fédéral**.*

ファニュエル・ホール内の**フェデラル様式**の集会所

FANEUIL HALL
"THE CRADLE OF LIBERTY"

"Erect a noble and complete structure . . . for the sole use and benefit and advantage of the town . . ." With these words, **Peter Faneuil** explained to his fellow citizens the principles that inspired the creation of this building, his gift to the city that had made him immensely wealthy. This dual-function building, with a **market** space on the ground floor and the **Assembly Hall** over it, established itself as the political and business center of Boston almost as soon as it was inaugurated in 1742—but it is also renowned as the "Cradle of Liberty" since it was host to the first mass citizens' assemblies that were destined to change the course of American history forever.

„Errichtet ein erlesenes und vollkommenes Bauwerk... allein für das Wohlergehen und zum Vorteil der Stadt..." So erklärte **Peter Faneuil** seinen Mitbürgern die Prinzipien, nach denen dieses Gebäude entstehen sollte. Es war seine Gabe an die Stadt, der er seinen Reichtum verdankte. Die Doppelfunktion des Baus mit einem **Marktraum** im Erdgeschoss und einer **Assembly Hall** (Versammlungshalle) darüber, ließ es bald nach der Einweihung (1742) zum politischen und geschäftlichen Zentrum Bostons werden. Es ist auch als *Cradle of Liberty* (Wiege der Freiheit) bekannt, denn hier fanden die ersten Bürgerversammlungen statt, die die Geschichte Amerikas für immer verändern sollten.

"Bâtir une noble et complète structure... aux seuls usage, profit et avantage de la ville..." Ainsi **Peter Faneuil** expliquait-il à ses compatriotes les principes qui lui avaient inspiré la construction de ce bâtiment, son cadeau à la ville qui avait fait de lui un homme immensément riche. Édifice à double fonction, offrant un **marché** couvert au rez-de-chaussée et un **Assembly Hall** au premier, Faneuil Hall s'affirma comme centre de la politique et des affaires dès son inauguration, en 1742. On l'appelle aussi le "Berceau de la Liberté" (*Cradle of Liberty*) car il abrita les premières assemblées de masse durant lesquelles le peuple fit changer le cours de l'histoire américaine à jamais.

ファニュエル・ホール － 『自由の揺籃』
「ボストン市の利益と進歩のために建設された優美で完璧な建物」。**ピーター・ファニュエル**は同胞のボストン市民に、この建物の建造に至った動因をこう説明している。彼が町へ寄贈したこの建物は彼に莫大な富をもたらした。この建物は二重の役割を持ち、一階は**ショッピングセンター**で、その上には**集会所**がある。1742年の落成後ほぼすぐにボストン市の政治と商取引きの中心として考えられるようになった。またアメリカ史の方向を決定した最初の市民大集会が開かれたことから、『自由の揺籃』という名称でも知られている。

PAUL REVERE HOUSE

The twelfth stop on the Freedom Trail introduces us to the private life of the midnight rider. The house in which Paul Revere lived from 1770 to 1780 stands at **19 North Square** in the old North End neighborhood. The North Square building was restored to its original aspect in 1907, and since then has been a public monument that preserves a slice of the everyday life of a hero of the American Revolution.

Der zwölfte Halt am Freedom Trail führt uns in das Privatleben des „Mitternachtsreiters" ein. Das Haus in dem Paul Revere von 1770 bis 1780 lebte, steht am **North Square 19** im alten North End. Das North Square Building wurde 1907 in seiner ursprünglichen Form restauriert und seit damals vermittelt dieses öffentliche Monument ein Stück alltäglichen Lebens eines Helden der Amerikanischen Revolution.

La douzième étape du Freedom Trail nous fait entrer, au **19 North Square**, chez le héros de la légendaire chevauchée nocturne. Paul Revere habita de 1770 à 1780 dans cette maison qui, restaurée en 1907, conserve son aspect originel. C'est aujourd'hui un monument public qui préserve une tranche de vie familiale d'un des héros de la Révolution américaine.

ポール・リヴィアの家　フリーダム・トレイル第12の停止地は、ポール・リヴィアの家だ。ここでは、『ミッドナイト・ライダー』として有名な彼の私生活を垣間見ることができる。リヴィアは1770年から1780年まで、旧ノース・エンドに近い**ノース・スクエア19番地**にたつこの家に住んだ。この家は1907年にオリジナルの姿に修復され、以来アメリカ独立革命の英雄リヴィアの日常生活の一部を垣間見ることができる史跡となった。

Statue of Paul Revere. This work, sculpted by Cyrus Dallin in 1885 and cast in bronze in 1940, stands at the center of the pleasant tree-lined boulevard linking the Old North Church and St. Stephen's Church.

Statue des Paul Revere. Diese Arbeit, 1885 von Cyrus Dallin modelliert und 1940 in Bronze gegossen, steht in der Mitte des dreispurigen Boulevards, welcher Old North Church und St. Stephen's Church verbindet.

Statue de Paul Revere. Cette œuvre, sculptée par Cyrus Dallin en 1885 et moulée en bronze en 1940, se tient au milieu de l'agréable boulevard ombragé qui relie Old North Church à St Stephen's Church.

ポール・リヴィア像. 1885年シールス・ダリンが彫刻し、1940年にブロンズで鋳造されたこの作品は、オールド・ノース教会とセント・ステファン教会を結ぶ美しい3車線の大通りの真ん中にたつ。

PAUL REVERE
(1734-1818)

Engraver, metalworker, patriot. Revere was the son of Huguenot colonists, and began his apprenticeship in his father's shop, smithing silver. Paul Revere is best remembered for his **Midnight Ride**. Legend has it that on the night of 18 April 1775, after having agreed on a lantern signal ("One if by land, two if by sea") from the bell tower of the **Old North Church**, Revere took off at breakneck speed on horseback to warn the towns of **Lexington** and **Concord** of the approach of the British troops. This exploit, celebrated in **Henry Wadsworth Longfellow's** famous poem (*The Midnight Ride of Paul Revere*), has become an integral part of American patriotic folklore. The silversmith of Boston well deserves his reputation as a hero of the American Revolution, having fought in the Continental Army until 1779, when he returned to his myriad professional activities and civic duties. In 1788 he opened a foundry specializing in bells and cannons, where the **King's Chapel** bell was cast. A few years later his interests turned to copper, and his sheets of this metal covered the dome of Bulfinch's new **State House** as well as the sides of the *USS Constitution*.

Der Kupferstecher, Metallhandwerker und Patriot Revere war Sohn von Hugenotten und Kolonisten. Er lernte als Silberschmied in der Werkstatt seines Vaters. An ihn erinnert man sich wegen seines **Midnight Ride** (Mitternachtsritt). Er soll in der Nacht des 18. April 1775 - nach einem Laternensignal vom Glockenturm der **Old North Church** („Einmal wenn über Land, zweimal wenn über See") - in halsbrecherischem Tempo losgeritten sein, um die Städte **Lexington** und **Concord** wegen des Anrückens der britischen Truppen zu warnen. Diese Tat wird in einem Gedicht von **Henry Wadsworth Longfellow** *(The Midnight Ride of Paul Revere)* gefeiert und gehört heute zur patriotischen Folklore. Der Silberschmied verdiente sich seinen Ruf als Held Amerikas außerdem, weil er bis 1779 in der Continental Army focht, danach griff er seine unzähligen Pflichten und Tätigkeiten wieder auf. 1788 gründete er eine Gießerei für Kanonen und Glocken, dort wurde die Glocke der **King's Chapel** gegossen. Kupferplatten aus seiner Werkstatt bedecken die Kuppel von Bulfinchs neuem **State House** und auch die Flanken des Schlachtschiffs *USS Constitution*.

Graveur et fondeur, fils de colons huguenots, Paul Revere commença son apprentissage dans l'atelier de son père, argentier. Patriote, il est surtout connu pour sa chevauchée nocturne légendaire: la **Midnight Ride**. On raconte que dans la nuit du 18 avril 1775, lorsqu'il aperçut le signal convenu (deux lanternes) en haut du clocher d'**Old North Church**, il sauta sur son cheval et partit à bride abattue avertir les habitants de **Lexington** et de **Concord** de l'arrivée de la flotte anglaise. Cet exploit, immortalisé par le poème de **Henry Wadsworth Longfellow** *The Midnight Ride of Paul Revere*, fait désormais partie intégrante du folklore patriotique américain. Paul Revere mérite aussi sa renommée de héros de la Révolution américaine pour avoir combattu dans l'armée coloniale jusqu'en 1779. Après quoi, il retrouva sa ville et ses multiples activités professionnelles et civiques. En 1788, il ouvrit une fonderie qui fabriquait canons et cloches – on lui doit la cloche de la **King's Chapel** – et, quelques années plus tard, se spécialisa dans le travail du cuivre: c'est lui qui réalisa les plaques de ce métal qui couvrent le dôme de la **New State House** de Charles Bulfinch, ainsi que celles qui permirent de blinder la frégate *Constitution*.

ポール・リヴィア((1734-1818年))　版画師、金属細工師そして愛国者。リヴィアはユグノーの入植者の息子で、銀細工師だった父親の工房で修行を始めた。ポール・リヴィアの名は**ミッドナイト・ライド**で有名だ。伝説では1775年4月18日の夜、英国軍の進路を知らせる**オールド・ノース教会**の鐘楼のランタンの合図を受けて(陸上攻撃は1回、海上攻撃は2回)、**レキシントンとコンコード**の町に警告するために馬で急行したという。**ヘンリー・ワズワース・ロングフェロウ**の有名な詩に謳われたこの英雄的な行為は、アメリカ愛国の伝説の一つだ。ボストンの一介の銀細工師だったリヴィアは、1779年まで植民地軍兵士として戦い、アメリカ革命運動の英雄として名声を獲得した。その後数多くの職業をこなし、公務を果たしていった。1788年には鐘と大砲を製造する特別な鋳造所を開設した。**キングス・チャペル**の鐘が製造されたのはここだ。数年後彼は銅に興味を持ちはじめ、ブルフィンチが設計した新**州庁舎**のドームや**USSコンスティテューション号**を覆う銅版を製造した。

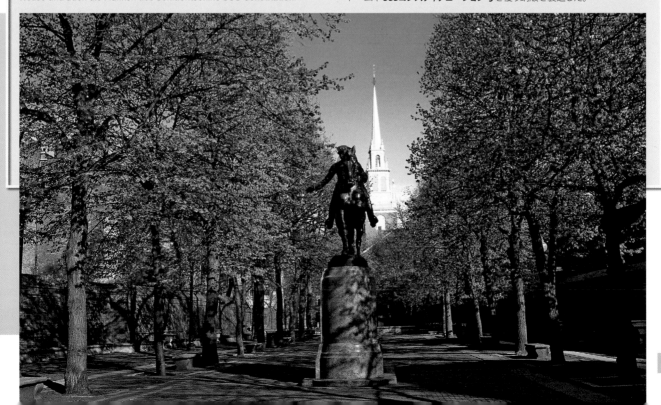

OLD NORTH CHURCH

Old North Church, or Christ Church, attributed to the architect **William Price**, is the second Anglican church built in Boston. It is best known as the church of the bell tower from which it is said that the imminent arrival of the British troops was signaled to **Paul Revere** on the night of his famous ride. The fine original bell tower was, however, destroyed by a hurricane in 1804 and was replaced with another designed by **Charles Bulfinch** in 1807; Bulfinch's tower was flattened by Hurricane Carol in 1954, but was rebuilt to the original design.

Die Old North Church oder Christ Church, dem Architekten **William Price** zugeschrieben, ist Bostons zweite anglikanische Kirche. Von ihrem Glockenturm wurde **Paul Revere** die unmittelbar bevorstehende Ankunft der britischen Truppen signalisiert, woraufhin er den berühmten Mitternachtsritt unternahm. Der elegante ursprüngliche Turm wurde 1804 von einem Hurrikan zerstört, den **Charles Bulfinch** 1807 durch einen anderen ersetzte. Bulfinchs Turm fiel wiederum dem Hurrikan Carol zum Opfer (1954), doch wurde er nach dem Originalentwurf erneuert.

Aussi appelée Christ Church, cette église attribuée à l'architecte **William Price** est la deuxième église anglicane bâtie à Boston. Elle est surtout célèbre pour son clocher d'où l'arrivée de la flotte britannique fut signalée à **Paul Revere** la nuit de sa chevauchée légendaire. Le joli clocher d'origine fut détruit par un ouragan en 1804 et remplacé par un autre, dû à l'architecte **Charles Bulfinch**, en 1807. Abattu à son tour, par l'ouragan Carol en 1954, ce clocher a été reconstruit à l'identique.

オールド・ノース教会

オールド・ノース教会はクライスト教会とも呼ばれる。設計者は**ウィリアム・プライス**と考えられている。ボストンでは2番目に古い英国国教会の教会だ。**ポール・リヴィア**がこの教会の鐘楼に掲げられたランタンの灯りを見て馬を走らせ、英国軍の襲来を防いだことは有名だ。美しいオリジナルの鐘楼は1804年のハリケーンで破壊されたため、1807年に**チャールズ・ブルフィンチ**設計による新しい鐘楼が建て直された。しかしブルフィンチの鐘楼も1954年のハリケーン「キャロル」の襲来で倒壊したため、オリジナルの形で再建された。

The second cemetery to be founded in Boston is located in the North End area. According to some sources, Copp's Hill takes its name from the shoemaker **William Copp** from whom the land was purchased in 1659; others, instead, argue that the name is a play on words from Corpse Hill. This ancient cemetery hosts the tombs of the **Mather family of preachers**, of **Edmund Harrt**, the builder of the *USS Constitution*, of **Robert Newman**, the Old North Church sexton who from the bell tower gave Paul Revere his signal to ride, and of **Prince Hall**, the founder of the first Black Masonic Lodge.

Le deuxième en date des cimetières de Boston se trouve dans le North End et était jadis situé au sommet de Copp's Hill. L'appellatif de cette colline viendrait, selon certains, du nom de William Copp, un cordonnier à qui le terrain fut acheté en 1659. Pour d'autres, il s'agirait d'un jeu de mots: une déformation de Corpse Hill (la Colline aux Cadavres). Ce très vieux cimetière abrite les tombes des **Mather**, une famille de prédicateurs, d'**Edmund Harrt**, constructeur de la *Constitution*, de **Robert Newman**, sacristain d'Old North Church qui, la nuit du 18 avril 1775, donna à Paul Revere le signal convenu du haut du clocher, et de **Prince Hall**, fondateur de la première loge maçonnique noire.

Der zweite in Boston gegründete Friedhof liegt im Gebiet von North End. Nach einigen Quellen heißt Copp's Hill nach dem Schumacher **William Copp**, von dem man 1659 das Land erwarb, andere behaupten, es sei ein Wortspiel um den Begriff Corpse Hill (Leichnam-Hügel). Dieser alte Friedhof enthält die Gräber der **Prediger-Familie Mather**, von **Edmund Harrt**, der das Schlachtschiff *USS Constitution* baute, von **Robert Newman**, dem Küster der Old North Church, welcher Paul Revere vom Glockenturm aus das Signal gab und von **Prince Hall**, dem Grunder der ersten Loge für Schwarze.

コップス・ヒル墓地

ボストンで2番目に古い墓地で、ノース・エンド地区に位置する。一説によるとコップス・ヒルという名称は、1659年にこの土地を売却した靴職人**ウィリアム・コップ**に由来する。またコープス・ヒル（死体の丘という意味）がなまってコップス・ヒルになったという説もある。いずれにしてもこの墓地には多くの名士が埋葬されている。説教者として有名な**マーサー一家**、*USS*コンスティテューション号を建造した**エドモント・ハート**、オールド・ノース教会の堂守で鐘楼からポール・リヴィアに合図を送った**ロバート・ニューマン**、フリーメーソン黒人ロッジの創設者**プリンス・ホール**などは特に有名だ。

Zwei Monate nach der Niederlage der Briten bei Concord und Lexington startete der General **William Howe** den Gegenangriff der britischen Armee. Sein Plan sah vor, die Stadt von den im Hafen ankernden Schiffen aus zu beschießen und auch von Charlestowns Hügeln Breed's und Bunker Hill, beide in strategischer Lage über Boston. Über dieses Vorhaben informiert befestigten die Kolonisten Breed's Hill für den Zusammenstoß mit den Briten. Die Schlacht nennt sich Battle of Bunker Hill, ereignete sich aber in Wirklichkeit auf dem Breed's Hill. Nach langem und blutigem Kampf zogen sich die Kolonisten zurück, weil ihnen die Munition ausging. Unter den Gefallenen der Continental Army beklagte man auch **General Joseph Warren**, ein Protagonist im politischen und sozialen Leben der Stadt. Sein Denkmal wurde von **Solomon Willard** entworfen und 1843 eingeweiht.

Deux mois après la défaite des Britanniques à Concord et Lexington, le général **William Howe** était prêt à lancer la contre-attaque. Son plan prévoyait de bombarder Boston du bord des vaisseaux ancrés dans le port et du haut des collines de Charlestown, Breed's et Bunker situées en position stratégique face à la ville. Prévenus, les colons fortifièrent Breed's Hill et se préparèrent à affronter l'adversaire. L'engagement, connu comme bataille de Bunker Hill, eut en fait lieu sur Breed's Hill. Ce fut un combat long et sanglant au terme duquel les colons furent contraints de battre en retraite faute de munitions. Parmi les morts de la milice coloniale se trouvait le **général Joseph Warren**, grande personnalité de la vie politique et sociale de Boston. Le monument commémoratif de la bataille, Bunker Hill Monument dû à **Solomon Willard**, fut inauguré en 1843.

BUNKER HILL

Two months after the British defeat at Concord and Lexington, General **William Howe** was ready to launch the counterattack by the British Army. His plan involved bombarding the city from the ships anchored in the port and from the two hills of Charlestown, Breed's and Bunker, in strategic positions facing Boston. Advised of these intentions, the colonists fortified Breed's Hill and prepared to meet the British troops; the encounter known in history as the Battle of Bunker Hill therefore actually took place on Breed's Hill. Following a long and bloody engagement, the colonists were forced to retreat when their ammunition ran out. Among the fallen in the ranks of the Continental Army was **General Joseph Warren**, a prominent figure in the political and social life of the city. The monument, designed by **Solomon Willard**, was dedicated in 1843.

バンカー・ヒル

コンコード・レキシントンの戦いで英国が惨敗した数ヵ月後、英国軍の**ウィリアム・ホウ**将軍は反撃を準備していた。彼の計画では、港に停泊中の船からと、チャールズタウンの2つの丘で、ちょうどボストンの向かい側の軍事的な要衝であるブリーズ・ヒルとバンカー・ヒルから町に砲撃を行う予定だった。彼の意図を知った植民地軍はブリーズ・ヒルの警備を固め、英国軍の攻撃に備えた。バンカー・ヒルの戦いという名で歴史に名高い戦闘は実はブリーズ・ヒルで起こったものだ。長期にわたる血生臭い戦闘の結果、砲弾が尽きた植民地軍は撤退を余儀なくされた。植民地軍の戦死兵の中には、ボストンの政界と社交界の大物**ジョゼフ・ワーレン**将軍もいた。1843年この場所には**ソロモン・ウィラード**が設計した記念塔が建てられた。

Bunker Hill Monument: *the statue of* **Colonel William Prescott**, *the valorous American commander whose order "Don't fire until you see the whites of their eyes" has remained in history.*

Bunker Hill Monument, *die Statue des* **Obersten William Prescott**, *des tapferen Kommandeurs, dessen Befehl „feuert nicht, bevor ihr das Weiße ihrer Augen seht" in die Geschichte einging.*

Bunker Hill Monument *et la statue du* **colonel William Prescott**, *valeureux commandant américain dont l'ordre "Ne tirez pas tant que vous ne verrez pas le blanc de leurs yeux" est passé à l'histoire.*

バンカー・ヒル記念塔:ウィリアム・プリスコット大佐の像。有能な指揮官で「敵の目が見えるまで発砲するな」という彼の言葉は有名だ。

USS CONSTITUTION

Affectionately known as **"Old Ironsides"**, USS *Constitution* is the oldest commissioned warship afloat in the world. Built in Edmund Hartt's shipyard in Boston, she cost the infant US Navy the sum of $302,718 and was launched on October 21, 1797. USS *Constitution* was one of six frigates requested by President George Washington and authorized by Congress in 1794, and was built to defend the American merchant fleet. She participated in two major campaigns: one in 1803-1805 against the corsairs of the North African coast, and the other in the War of 1812 against the British.

The most important of USS *Constitution*'s battles was her encounter with HMS **Guerriere** off the coast of Nova Scotia in 1812. When cannonballs appeared to bounce off her thick oaken hull, a sailor is reported to have exclaimed Huzza! Her sides are made of iron, giving rise to her nickname. She defeated other enemy ships during the war and gained national acclaim for herself and her crew. In 1830, rumors spread that the navy might scrap the ship. A poem entitled "Old Ironsides" by Harvard student Oliver Wendell Holmes, Jr. helped to change any such plans. In the years that followed, USS *Constitution* sailed the seas to combat the slave trade and served as a training ship in several places. She has been refitted several times including 1927-1931 thanks to the generosity of America's school children, and in 1992-1996 in preparation for her bicentennial which culminated in her sailing under her own power for the first time in 116 years on July 21, 1997. Each year, during Fourth of July celebrations, USS *Constitution* makes a ceremonial voyage around the Port of Boston.

Unter dem liebevollen Namen **"Old Ironsides"** (alte Eisenhaut) bekannt, gilt USS *Constitution* als das älteste in Dienst gestellte, noch schwimmende Kriegsschiff der Welt. Das in der Werft Edmund Hartt in Boston gebaute Schiff kostete die damals in den Kinderschuhen steckende US-Marine 302.718 Dollar, am 21. Oktober 1797 lief es vom Stapel. Die USS *Constitution* war eine von sechs Fregatten, die sich Präsident George Washington vom Kongress bewilligen ließ (1794), um die Handelsflotte Amerikas zu beschützen. Sie war an zwei wichtigen Kampagnen beteiligt, 1803-1805 gegen die Piraten der nordafrikanischen Küste und 1812 im Krieg gegen die Briten. Ihre bedeutendste Schlacht bestand die USS *Constitution* gegen die HMS **Guerrière** vor der Küste Neuschottlands (1812). Als die Kanonenkugeln von ihrem dicken Eichenrumpf abprallten, soll ein Seeman hurra! gerufen haben. Wegen seiner eisernen Flanken erhielt das Schiff den bereits erwähnten Spitznamen. Es besiegte während des Krieges noch weitere feindliche Schiffe, zu seinem Ruhm und dem der Mannschaft. 1830 hieß es, dass die Kriegsmarine die Fregatte abwracken wollte, aber das Gedicht „Old Ironsides" des Havard-Studenten Oliver Wendell Holmes Jr. trug dazu bei, diese Pläne aufzugeben. In den folgenden Jahren befuhr die USS *Constitution* alle Meere, um den Sklavenhandel zu bekämpfen und diente an verschiedenen Orten als Ausbildungsschiff. Sie wurde mehrfach erneuert, darunter auch von 1927-1931, dank der Großzügigkeit amerikanischer Schulkinder und dann nochmals von 1992 bis 1996, um sie auf die Zweihundertjahrfeier der USA vorzubereiten. Jedes Jahr, anlässlich des 4. Julis, umrundet die USS *Constitution* in feierlicher Fahrt den Hafen von Boston.

Affectueusement surnommé **"Old Ironsides"** (Vieux bordages de tôle), l'**USS *Constitution*** est le plus ancien bâtiment de guerre du monde encore en service. Construit par les chantiers navals d'Edmund Harrt à Boston, il coûta à la toute jeune US Navy la somme de 302.718 $ et fut baptisé le 21 octobre 1797. C'était l'une des six frégates dont la construction, demandée par le président George Washington, fut votée par le Congrès en 1794 afin d'assurer la protection de la marine marchande américaine. Le *Constitution* participa à deux grandes campagnes: en 1803-1805 contre les corsaires des côtes nord-africaines et durant la guerre de 1812 contre les Anglais. Il livra une de ses plus grandes batailles en 1812, au large de la Nouvelle-Écosse, contre le HMS ***Guerrière***. On dit qu'un marin poussa un Hourrah! lorsque les premiers boulets de l'ennemi rebondirent contre l'épaisse coque de chêne dont les bordages étaient revêtus de tôle d'acier, d'où son surnom. Les combats victorieux livrés durant cette guerre valurent au vaisseau et à son équipage les honneurs nationaux. En 1830, le bruit courut que la Marine voulait le démolir mais le poème "Old Ironsides" d'Oliver Wendell Holmes Jr., étudiant à Harvard, aida à l'en dissuader. Dans les années qui suivirent, le *Constitution* sillonna les mers en combattant les négriers puis servit de navire-école. Il fut plusieurs fois réparé et remis à neuf: en 1927-1931, grâce à la générosité des écoliers américains, et en 1992-1996 en vue de la fête de son bicentenaire au cours de laquelle, le 21 juillet 1997, l'USS *Constitution* navigua à la voile pour la première fois sans assistance depuis 116 ans. Tous les ans, lors des commémorations du 4 juillet, l'USS *Constitution* fait solennellement le tour du port de Boston.

A period painting of the **USS Constitution** after she dismasted the British warship **HMS Guerriere** in battle.

Peinture d'époque représentant la **USS Constitution** après son combat contre la **HMS Guerrière** qu'il démâta.

Ein zeitgenössisches Gemälde mit dem Sieg der **USS Constitution** über das britische Kriegsschiff **HMS Guerrière**.

戦闘で英国軍艦HMSゲリエール号を破った**USSコンスティテューション号**を描いた当時の絵

　　『オールド・アイロンサイズ』の愛称で親しまれている**USSコンスティテューション号**は、就役中の軍艦としては世界最古のものだ。エドモンド・ハートが所有するボストンの造船所で建造されたこの船に、創設されて間もないアメリカ海軍は302,718ドルという膨大な金額を支払った。進水式が執り行われたのは、1797年10月21日だ。USSコンスティテューション号は、ジョージ・ワシントン大統領の要請を受けて1794年の国会の承認された6隻のフリゲート船の一つで、アメリカ商船を保護する目的で建造された。1803年から1806年にかけて行なわれた北アフリカ沿岸の海賊との戦闘そして1812年の対英国戦という、2つの大遠征にも参加した。その中でも特に有名な戦闘は、1812年ニュー・スコットランド沖でHMS**ゲリエール号**と交わした激戦だ。USSコンスティテューション号のオーク材でできた厚い船体が、発射された敵の大砲をはね返したかのように見えた時には「ハザー」という大歓声が上がった、と一人の水兵が記録に残しているほどだ。船体の側面が鉄でできているため『オールド・アイロンサイズ』というニックネームで呼ばれるようになった。対英国戦中はその他にも数多くの敵船を撃破したので、USSコンスティテューション号とその乗り組み員は国民的英雄としてアメリカ全土の歓呼を浴びた。ところが1830年、アメリカ海軍がUSSコンスティテューション号の解体を計画しているという噂が立った。ハーヴァード大学の若い学生オリヴァー・ウェンデル・ホルムズJrは『オールド・アイロンサイズ』という題の詩を書き、そのお陰でUSSコンスティテューション号は悲惨な運命を逃れることができた。その後USSコンスティテューション号は奴隷貿易を阻止するなど軍艦として活躍したり、訓練船として世界の海を航行した。アメリカ全国の就学児童の寄付で1927年から1931年にかけて行なわれた修復を含めて、数回の修復工事が行われた。また1992年から1996年にかけて二百周年記念準備のために再度大掛かりな修復が施されて、ついに1997年7月21日、116年ぶりに自力で航行を果たすことができた。毎年7月4日のアメリカ独立記念日には、USSコンスティテューション号はボストン湾を一周する。

THE HARBOR

The spectacular **Rowe's Wharf**, the main landing for yachts and ferryboats, dominates the new Port of Boston, greeting visitors coming into the city by water from Logan Airport. The 15-story building designed in 1987 by **Skidmore, Owings & Merril** is home to a hotel, a marina, apartments, office suites, and shops. Don't miss the panoramas from the **Forester Rotunda**, on the 9th floor. Boston was at one time a peninsula connected to the mainland by a narrow isthmus, but with the passing of the years its coastline was modified by landfills along the shores. The material came mostly from two of the three hills of Boston's original **Trimountain**, of which only Beacon Hill remains.

DER HAFEN

Rowe's Wharf ist der Hauptanlegeplatz von Jachten und Fährbooten im Hafen von Boston. Hier landet der Besucher, der vom Logan Airport auf dem Wasserweg ankommt. Das dortige 15 Stockwerke hohe Gebäude, 1987 von **Skidmore, Owings & Merril** entworfen, enthält ein Hotel, eine Marina, Wohnungen, Büroräume und Geschäfte. Man gönne sich den Panoramablick von der **Forester Rotunda** im 9. Stock. Boston war zunächst eine Halbinsel, die über eine Landzunge mit dem Festland verbunden war. Doch die Küste veränderte sich, weil man längs des Ufers Auffüllungen vornahm. Das Material dafür stammt von den **Trimountain** genannten drei Hügeln, von denen sich nur der Beacon Hill erhalten hat.

LE PORT

Le spectaculaire complexe de **Rowe's Wharf**, quai principal où accostent navettes et yachts, domine le nouveau port de Boston et salue les visiteurs qui, de Logan Airport, arrivent à Boston par la mer. Ce complexe de 15 étages, construit en 1987 par **Skidmore, Owings & Merril**, comprend une marina, un hôtel, des appartements, des bureaux et des magasins. Le panorama du haut de la **Forester Rotunda**, au 9ème étage, est superbe.
Boston était jadis une péninsule reliée à la terre ferme par un petit isthme. Au fil des siècles sa forme a considérablement changé car des terrains ont été gagnés sur la mer grâce, entre autres, au matériau provenant de deux des trois collines du groupe de **Trimountain** ou Tremont dont il ne reste que Beacon Hill.

ハーバー

美しい**ロウズ・ワーフ**は新ボストン湾を支配する主要なヨットやフェリーの停泊所で、ローガン空港から水上フェリーを使って市内に入る玄関口だ。**スキドモア**、**オウイング**、**メリル**の３人が1987年に共同設計したこの15階建てビルは、ホテル、マリーナ、アパート、オフィスや店舗が置かれている。９階にある**フォレスター・ロトンダ**からのパノラマは絶景だ。昔ボストンは細い地峡で本島と結ばれた半島だったが、長い間に海岸沿いに徐々に土砂が溜まっていったため、海岸線は大きく変ってしまった。この土砂はボストンの**トリマウンテン**と呼ばれる３つの丘のうち２つから崩れてきたものだ。結局、丘として残ったのはビーコン・ヒルだけだ。

NEW ENGLAND AQUARIUM

Primary attractions at this huge aquarium (with about 2000 species of marine fauna) at the **Central Wharf** are the **Penguin Pool**, with three different species (African, Rockhopper, and Blue), the **Giant Ocean Tank** that recreates the habitat of the tropical seas, and the **Freshwater Gallery** illustrating freshwater ecosystems. At the **Sea Lion Pool** in the floating **Discovery** pavilion, you'll see how these animals live and are trained. One priority aim of the aquarium is to teach the public how to interact with the animals and their habitat, as in **Edge of the Sea** and in the veterinary section.

Hauptattraktionen dieses gewaltigen Aquariums mit seinen etwa 2000 Spezies von Seegetier sind am **Central Wharf** der **Penguin Pool** mit drei Pinguin-Arten, der **Giant Ocean Tank**, welcher die Tropischen Meere rekonstruiert und die **Freshwater Gallery**, welche die Süßwasser-Ecosysteme veranschaulicht. Am **Sea Lion Pool** im schwimmenden **Discovery**-Pavillon sieht man, wie die Seelöwen leben und trainiert werden. Aufgabe des Aquariums ist es, dem Publikum zu zeigen, wie man mit den Tieren und ihrem Ambiente in eine korrekte Beziehung tritt, so zu sehen in **Edge of the Sea** und der Veterinärabteilung.

Boreal sea stars and a sea turtle.

Seesterne des Nordmeeres und eine Meeresschildkröte.

Étoiles des mers boréales et une tortue marine.

ボーリアルヒトデと
海がめ

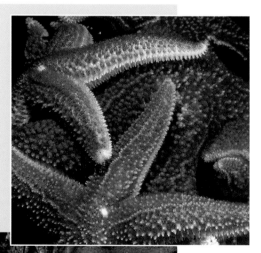

Cet immense aquarium, accueillant quelque 2000 espèces de la faune marine, est situé sur **Central Wharf** et offre de grandes attractions, comme le **Penguin Pool** où évoluent trois espèces de manchots (manchot du cap, gorfou sauteur et manchot bleu), le **Giant Ocean Tank**, bassin océanique géant où l'on a reconstitué l'habitat des mers tropicales, la **Freshwater Gallery** qui présente les écosystèmes d'eau douce et le **Sea Lion Pool** dont le pavillon flottant **Discovery** permet de voir les otaries de tout près. L'aquarium s'est fixé entre autres grands objectifs d'apprendre au public à interagir avec les animaux et leur habitat; en particulier, grâce à son bassin **Edge of the Sea** (Bord de mer) et à sa section vétérinaire.

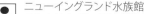 ニューイングランド水族館
　セントラル・ワーフにあるこの巨大な水族館(約2000種類の水中生物がいる)には、3種類のペンギン(アフリカ、ロックホッパー、ブルー)が飼われている**ペンギン・プール**、熱帯の海の生態を再現した**ジャイアント・オーシャン・タンク**、淡水の生態系を知ることができる**フレッシュウォーター・ギャラリー**などがある。**ディスカヴァリー・パヴィリオン**の**アシカ・プール**ではアシカの生態と訓練の様子を見ることができる。水族館の主な目的の一つは、水棲動物やその生態系と人間がどのように共存していくかを教えることだ。館内の**エッジ・オヴ・ザ・シー**や獣医学部門ではそのような教育活動も行われている。

BOSTON CHILDREN'S MUSEUM

The exhibits at the Children's Museum revolve around four major themes: the arts, science, technology, and culture. On the subject of the arts, one of the "musts" is the splendid collection of toys through history in the **Hall of Toys**, and, in the performing arts section, the **KidStage**. The **Science Playground** is a huge laboratory where children can experiment with science while playing. **New Balance Climb** is a labyrinth that stimulates children's sense of orientation in complex spaces. In the **Construction Zone**, kids can explore the technologies used at building sites. And finally, the cultural section features the **Japanese House** and **Boston Black**, which explains the role of the Black community in Boston history and invites children to reflect on such themes as race and cultural identity.

子供博物館

子供博物館は、芸術、科学、技術、文化という4大テーマを中心に展示が行われている。博物館の一つの『目玉』である**ホール・オヴ・トーイズ**には、素晴らしい玩具のコレクションが年代ごとに展示されている。**キッドステージ**は芸術を体験するコーナーだ。また**サイセンス・プレイグラウンド**は、遊びながら科学実験ができる巨大な研究室だ。ニュー・バランス・クライムは複雑な空間で子供たちの方向感覚を養う一種の迷路だ。**コンストラクション・ゾーン**では建築現場で使われる技術を学ぶことができる。文化部門では**日本家屋**やボストン史における黒人コミュニティの役割を紹介する**ボストン・ブラック**などがあり、子供たちが人種や文化上のアイデンティティについて考える機会を与えている。

Das Kindermuseum behandelt vier Themenkreise, Künste, Wissenschaft, Technologie und Kultur. In der **Hall of Toys** in der Kunstabteilung sieht man die historische Entwicklung des Spielzeugs. In der Abteilung Performing Arts wurde die Kinderbühne **KidStage** eingerichtet. Der **Science Playground** ist ein großes Laboratorium, wo Kinder beim Spiel mit der Naturwissenschaft in Kontakt kommen. **New Balance Climb** ist ein Labyrinth, das den Orientierungssinn der Kinder stimulieren soll. In der **Construction Zone** erleben die Kinder die Technologien der Baustellen. Schließlich findet man in der Kulturabteilung das **Japanese House** und **Boston Black**. Letzteres erklärt die Rolle der Schwarzen in Bostons Geschichte und lädt die Kinder dazu ein, über ethnische Zugehörigkeit und kulturelle Identität nachzudenken.

Les grands thèmes des expositions de ce musée dédié aux enfants sont au nombre de quatre: les arts, les sciences, la technologie et la culture. Parmi les "must" du musée, signalons sa collection splendide de jouets de tous les temps (**Hall of Toys**) et, côté arts du spectacle, la scène des enfants (**KidStage**). Et puis, le **Science Playground**, un gigantesque laboratoire-terrain de jeux où les enfants découvrent les sciences en s'amusant, et le **New Balance Climb**, un labyrinthe conçu pour développer le sens de l'orientation des petits. Et encore, la **Construction Zone**, où ils peuvent découvrir les technologies employées dans le bâtiment. Enfin, la section culture présente le Japon avec **Japanese House** et l'histoire de la ville avec **Boston Black** qui explique aux enfants le rôle joué par la communauté Noire, tout en suscitant une réflexion sur les questions raciales et d'identité culturelle.

Hood Statue: A 40-foot milk bottle serves as an ice cream stand.

Hood Statue, eine mehr als 12 m hohe Milchflasche dient als Eiskiosk.

Hood Statue: une bouteille de lait haute de 12 m où l'on vend des glaces.

フッド・スタチュ:
高さ40フィートのミルク缶の形をしたアイスクリーム・スタンド

BOSTON TEA PARTY

Despite the colonists' protests against the heavy duties imposed by the **Tea Act**, George III King of England sent three ships loaded with tea to Boston. When the ships entered the harbor in early December 1773, the citizenry, led by **Samuel Adams**, immediately mobilized and demanded that the tea be sent back whence it came. Royal Governor **Thomas Hutchinson** refused to accept this solution. Following an animated meeting at the **Old South Meeting House** on the night of **16 December 1773**, a group of Patriots thinly disguised as Mohawk Indians and encouraged by a large crowd of Bostonians boarded the **Dartmouth**, the **Beaver**, and the **Eleanor** and dumped 90,000 pounds of tea (for a value of about £9000) overboard into Boston Harbor. Boston had by this time been individuated as the hotbed of anti-British resistance it was, and for this reason its trading port was closed, the city was put under martial law, and the capital of Massachusetts was transferred to Salem. After much intercolonial correspondence, the **First Continental Congress** met in Philadelphia in September 1774 to coordinate concerted action by the colonies. The Boston Tea Party has gone down in history as the spark that set off the American War of Independence.

Trotz der energischen Proteste der Kolonisten gegen die hohen Teesteuern des **Tea Act**, sandte König Georg III. von England drei mit Tee beladene Schiffe nach Boston. Als die Schiffe Anfang Dezember 1773 in den Hafen segelten, geriet die von **Samuel Adams** angeführte Bürgerschaft sofort in Aufruhr und verlangte den Rücktransport des Tees. Der königliche Gouverneur **Thomas Hutchinson** wies diese Forderung zurück. Nach einer stürmischen Versammlung im **Old South Meeting House** am Abend des **16. Dezembers 1773**, verkleidete sich eine Gruppe von Patrioten als Mohikaner und von den Bostonern angefeuert, enterten sie die Schiffe **Dartmouth**, **Beaver** und **Eleanor** und warfen 40.823 kg Tee mit einem Wert von etwa 9000 Pfund Sterling in das Hafenbecken. Damit galt Boston als die Brutstätte der antibritischen Kräfte, der Handelshafen wurde geschlossen, die Stadt unterlag dem Kriegsrecht und man erklärte Salem zur neuen Hauptstadt von Massachusetts. Nach langen Beratungen zwischen den Kolonien trat im September 1774 in Philadelphia der **Erste Kontinentale Kongress** zusammen, um die Handlungen der Kolonien zu koordinieren. Die Boston Tea Party gilt in der Geschichtsschreibung als die Initialzündung für den amerikanischen Unabhängigkeitskrieg.

*The **Boston Beaver II** is a faithful reproduction of one of the ships assailed by the Patriots.*

Boston Beaver II *ist die Nachbildung eines der Schiffe, die von den Patrioten geentert wurden.*

*Le **Boston Beaver II**, fidèle reproduction d'un des navires britanniques pris d'assaut par les patriotes.*

ボストン・ビーヴァー2号はボストン茶会事件の舞台となった船の1隻を忠実に再現したものだ。

En dépit des vives protestations et du boycotte des colons en réponse aux taxes d'importation imposées par le **Tea Act**, le roi d'Angleterre, George III, envoya trois navires chargés de thé à Boston. Dès que ceux-ci entrèrent dans le port, début décembre 1773, la population, menée par **Samuel Adams**, se mobilisa et exigea qu'ils repartent d'où ils venaient. Le gouverneur royal, **Thomas Hutchinson**, refusa. Il s'ensuivit un rassemblement immédiat des Bostoniens à l'**Old South Meeting House** qui, dans la nuit du **16 décembre 1773**, soutinrent l'action des patriotes. Déguisés en Indiens Mohawks, ceux-ci assaillirent le **Dartmouth**, le **Beaver** et le l'**Eleanor** et en jetèrent la cargaison par-dessus bord (plus de 40 tonnes de thé d'une valeur d'environ 9000 £). Déjà connue comme étant le foyer de la résistance antibritannique, Boston fut durement sanctionnée: soumise à la loi martiale, son port de commerce fut fermé et la capitale du Massachusetts transférée à Salem. Réuni à Philadelphie en septembre 1774, après avoir été dûment préparé, le **Premier Congrès Continental** décida d'une action de lutte commune. La Boston Tea Party devait passer à l'histoire comme l'étincelle qui amorça la guerre d'Indépendance.

ボストン茶会事件

茶条例で課された重税に対する植民地の抵抗にもかかわらず、英国王ジョージ3世はボストンに茶を陸揚げしようと3隻の船を派遣した。1773年12月初旬に船がボストンに入港すると、**サミュエル・アダムス**率いる市民団はただちに撤退を要求した。しかし英国から派遣された**トーマス・ハッチンソン**提督は、その要求を拒否して陸揚げを強行しようとした。**1773年12月16日**の夜、**オールド・サウス集会所**で活発な討論が行われた結果、モホーク・インディアンに変装した愛国者たちは、ボストン市民の群集に応援されながら、港に碇泊中の3隻の船**ダートマウス**、**ビーヴァー**、**エレオノーラ**に乗り込み、90,000ポンドの茶(約£9,000の価値)をボストン湾に投げ捨てた。この事件以来、反英抵抗運動の温床として見なされたボストンに対して、英国政府はボストン港閉鎖をはじめとする弾圧的諸条約をもって応え、マサチューセッツの州都もサーレムに移された。植民地間では度重なる応答が繰り返されたが、結局植民地間の方針をまとめるめ1774年9月フィラデルフィアで**第1回大陸会議**が開催された。ボストン茶会事件はアメリカを独立戦争に導いた歴史的に重大な事件といえる。

QUINCY MARKET

Adjacent to Faneuil Hall, founded in 1823 by the second Mayor of Boston **Josiah Quincy,** the square was Boston's traders favorite marketplace throughout the 19th century. The ancient structure was restored in the 20th century; today's market counts three pavilions: **North, South**, and **Quincy**. The central **Quincy Pavilion** is the most spectacular from the architectural point of view, thanks to its Doric-style colonnades and the dome above the center rotunda. It is home to a great number of restaurants offering specialties of international cuisine; in the flanking buildings are boutiques, furniture stores, and many large chain stores like Gap and Banana Republic.

Neben der Faneuil Hall ließ 1823 der zweite Bürgermeister von Boston, **Josiah Quincy** diesen Platz anlegen, im 19. Jh. der beliebteste Marktplatz der Kaufleute Bostons. Die alte Anlage wurde im 20. Jh. restauriert, an dem heutigen Markt stehen drei Pavillons, der **Nord-**, der **Süd-** und der **Quincy-Pavillon**. Der zentrale Quincy-Pavillon ist von der Architektur her besonders auffällig, er hat einen dorischen Portikus und über der Rotunde erhebt sich eine Kuppel. Im Inneren gibt es viele Restaurants mit internationalen Spezialitäten. In den Seitengebäuden findet man Boutiquen, Möbelgeschäfte und Filialen von Läden wie Gap und Banana Republic.

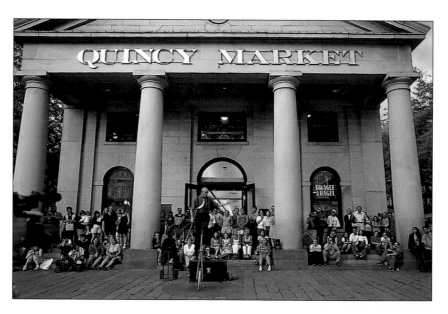

The rotunda in the **interior** and the crowd around the market building.

*Die Rotunde im **Inneren** und die Menschenmenge rings um das Marktgebäude.*

*La rotonde vue de l'**intérieur** et l'animation autour des anciennes halles.*

円形建築物の**内部**とマーケットの建物の周りの群集

Adjacentes à Faneuil Hall, les anciennes halles, fondées en 1823 par le second maire de Boston **Josiah Quincy**, fut le centre bostonien du négoce et des affaires tout au long du XIXe siècle. Actuellement, le Quincy Market, dont les bâtiments anciens furent restaurés au XXe siècle, comprend trois pavillons: **North**, **South** et, au milieu, **Quincy**. Le **Quincy Pavilion** est le plus spectaculaire au plan de l'architecture avec ses colonnades doriques et sa rotonde centrale coiffée d'un dôme. Il abrite désormais des restaurants proposant des spécialités de la cuisine internationale tandis que dans les deux autres bâtiments se trouvent boutiques, marchands de meubles et plusieurs grands magasins, dont ceux des chaînes Gap et Banana Republic.

クインシー・マーケット
　1823年ボストン２代目市長**ジョシュア・クインシー**が建設したファニュエル・ホールの隣にあるこの広場は、19世紀全般にわたってボストン商人たちが好んだ市場として知られている。昔の建物は20世紀に修復された。現在のマーケットは**ノース**、**サウス**、**クインシー**の３つの建物からなる。中央の**クインシー・パヴィリオン**は、ドリス式柱廊と中央の円形建築物を飾るドームが際立つ、建築上最も見ごたえがある作品だ。建物内には数多くのレストランがあり、世界中の料理を楽しめる。両脇の建物にはブティック、家具屋をはじめガップやバナナ・パブリックなどの大型チェーン店も置かれている。

CUSTOM HOUSE TOWER

Boston's first skyscraper (at 496 ft), the tower of the **Old Custom House** (1849) was raised in 1915 to meet the port's new needs. At the time, it was Boston's showiest building, and today its elegant figure still stands out among the modern buildings surrounding it on the waterfront panorama.

Bostons erster Wolkenkratzer (an die 151 m hoch) ist der Turm des **Old Custom House** (1849), er wurde 1915 zum Nutzen des Hafens gebaut. Damals war er das auffälligste Gebäude Bostons, aber auch heute noch behauptet er sich zwischen den modernen Architekturen an der Wasserfront.

Premier gratte-ciel de Boston (151 m), la tour des anciennes douanes – **Old Custom House** (1849) – fut construite en 1915 pour répondre aux besoins du nouveau port. Avec ses 30 étages, elle se targua à l'époque d'être le building le plus voyant de Boston. Aujourd'hui, sa silhouette élégante se distingue toujours parmi les gratte-ciel modernes qui l'entourent sur le Waterfront.

カスタム・ハウス・タワー
旧カスタム・ハウス(1849年)のタワーは、1915年に建築されたボストン初の超高層ビル(496フィート)で、当時ボストンで最も目立つ建物だった。近代的なビル群に周りを囲まれた現在も、その優美な姿はウォーターフロントの中で際立っている。

UNION OYSTER HOUSE

Inaugurated in Union Street in 1826, the Union Oyster House is universally known as the oldest US restaurant to have worked without pause down to our day. Over its long career, its patrons have included many historical exponents of American politics, such as **John Fitzgerald Kennedy.**

Das Union Oyster House in der Union Street gilt als das älteste Restaurant der USA, es bietet seit 1826 bis heute ohne Unterbrechung seine Dienste an. Zu seinen Stammkunden zählten viele herausragende Persönlichkeiten der amerikanischen Politik wie z.B. **John Fitzgerald Kennedy.**

Cette table célèbre de Union Street est universellement connue comme étant le plus ancien restaurant américain à être resté ouvert sans interruption depuis son inauguration, en 1826. Au fil de cette longue carrière, sa clientèle a compté de nombreuses personnalités du monde politique américain, dont **John Fitzgerald Kennedy**.

ユニオン・オイスター・ハウス
1826年ユニオン・ストリートに開店したユニオン・オイスター・ハウスは、合衆国最古のレストランとして有名だ。開店以来休みなく現在まで活動を続けている。この店はその長い歴史の中で、**ジョン・フィッツジェラルド・ケネディ**などアメリカ政界の大物をオーナーに迎えたこともある。

OLD CITY HALL

🇺🇸 Old City Hall was the seat of city government from the year of its inauguration, 1865, through 1969 when it was transformed into a multipurpose center hosting organizations, offices, and restaurants. Outside this notable example of historic preservation and adaptive reuse of the ancient urban fabric stands the **statue of Benjamin Franklin**, with bas-reliefs recalling the great Bostonian's multifarious doings.

🇩🇪 Die Old City Hall diente vom Jahr ihrer Einweihung (1865) bis 1969 als Rathaus, dann verwandelte man sie in einen Vielzweckbau, in dem Gesellschaften, Büros und Restaurants zu finden sind. Außerhalb des Gebäudes – ein lobenswertes Beispiels für Bewahrung und Anpassung alten Baubestandes – erhebt sich das **Denkmal Benjamin Franklins**. Reliefs erinnern an die mannigfaltigen Taten dieses großen Bostoner Bürgers.

🇫🇷 Ce beau bâtiment fut le siège de l'administration municipale, à compter de son inauguration en 1865 jusqu'en 1969, date à laquelle il fut reconverti en centre polyvalent (sièges d'associations, bureaux, restaurants). Il s'agit d'un remarquable exemple de protection et de reconversion du patrimoine historique de Boston. En face, la **statue de Benjamin Franklin** porte sur son socle des bas-reliefs évoquant la vie de ce Bostonien hors pair.

🇯🇵 旧市庁舎
旧市庁舎は創設時の1865年から1969年まで市の行政府が置かれていた。その後、多目的センターに変り、現在は各種機関、オフィス、レストランなどがある。古い史跡でありながら、その構造を再利用して現在のニーズに適応させたものだ。旧市庁舎の外にたつのは、**ベンジャミン・フランクリン**の像だ。ボストン生まれのこの偉人の多彩な才能が浅浮き彫りで記されている。

*The **Benjamin Franklin** (Boston, 1706-1790) statue in the courtyard.*

*Die Statue **Benjamin Franklins** (Boston, 1706-1790) im Innenhof.*

*La statue de **Benjamin Franklin** (Boston, 1706-1790) dans la cour.*

*中庭にたつ**ベンジャミン・フランクリン**(ボストン 1706-1790年)の像*

BOSTON'S
OLD
CITY HALL
1865 ~ 1969

RENOVATED AND MANAGED
BY
ARCHITECTURAL HERITAGE
FOUNDATION

45

POST OFFICE SQUARE

This modern plaza is a pleasant green island in today's Financial District. Created in the late 1980's, Post Office Square is the fruit of a compromise between the city authorities, who wanted a parking lot, and the area's shopkeepers, who campaigned for a park. No expense was spared for realization of the project: the park was designed down to the last detail (like the granite-paved paths and small squares, the fountain, sculptures, and a colonnade), as was the parking area complete with a car-wash facility, a shoe-maker's shop, and rest rooms. Despite the high cost, the complex breathed new life into the area—and also won quite a number of awards!

Dieser Platz ist eine gefällige grüne Insel inmitten des Financial District. Der in den späten 1980er Jahren angelegte Post Office Square entstand aus einem Kompromiss zwischen der Stadtverwaltung, die hier einen Parkplatz anlegen wollte und den Ladenbesitzern, welche sich für einen Park stark machten. Man scheute für dieses Projekt keine Ausgaben (Granitpflaster auf den Wegen, kleine Plätzchen, ein Brunnen, Skulpturen und eine Kolonnade) und der Parkplatz wurde mit Waschanlage für Autos, einem Schumacherladen und Toiletten vervollständigt. Abgesehen von den hohen Kosten setzte der Platz aber einen neuen Akzent und gewann sogar mehrere Auszeichnungen.

Cet îlot de verdure aménagé au milieu du quartier des affaires est très agréable. Créé à la fin des années 1980, il est le fruit d'un compromis entre la Municipalité, qui désirait y construire un parking, et les commerçants du quartier qui se battirent pour avoir un parc. On ne lésina pas sur la dépense pour mettre en œuvre ce projet, soigné jusque dans le moindre détail, aussi bien s'agissant du parc (allées et petits squares pavés de granite, fontaines, sculptures, colonnade) que pour le grand parking souterrain (station de lavage, toilettes). En dépit de son coût, le complexe, dont le projet a remporté plusieurs prix, a insufflé une nouvelle vie au quartier.

ポスト・オフィス・スクエア
この近代的な広場は、今日ファイナンシャル・ディストリクトの緑の楽園をなす。1980年代後半に建設されたポスト・オフィス・スクエアは、駐車場用地への転用を計画していた市の行政府と公園の建設運動を行っていた地域の商店主たちの折衝の結果誕生したものだ。この計画を実現するために莫大な費用が使われた。公園は細部まで丹念に建築され（花崗岩の石畳の通りや空間、噴水、彫像、柱廊など）、駐車場には洗車設備、靴屋、トイレなどが完備されている。高額な経費にもかかわらず、この建物は周辺地域に活性化を図り、多くの賞も受賞した。

HOLOCAUST MEMORIAL

The monument in memory of the Holocaust stands—significantly—on the Freedom Trail. Its **six glass columns** recall the holocaust of 6 million Jews and the 6 major Nazi concentration camps: Majdanek, Chelmno, Sobibor, Treblinka, Belzec, and Auschwitz-Birkenau. The Memorial, designed by Stanley Saitowitz/Natoma Architects (1991), was erected thanks to action by a group of Nazi camp survivors who began new lives in Boston, and to the sponsorship of more than 3000 organizations and individuals.

Dieses Holocaust-Mahnmal erhebt sich am Freedom Trail. **Sechs Glassäulen** erinnern an den Tod von 6 Millionen Juden in den 6 größten Konzentrationslagern der Nazis, Majdanek, Chelmno, Sobibor, Treblinka, Belzec und Auschwitz-Birkenau. Von den Architekten Stanley Saitowitz/Natoma im Jahr 1991entworfen, ist es der Initiative einiger Überlebender der Konzentrationslager zu verdanken, die in Boston ein neues Leben begannen. Mehr als 3000 Körperschaften und Einzelpersonen leisteten als Sponsoren ihren Beitrag.

Le saisissant monument qui commémore l'holocauste se dresse sur Freedom Trail. Ses **six colonnes de verre** évoquent les 6 millions de juifs victimes de l'holocauste et les 6 grands camps d'extermination nazis: Majdanek, Chelmno, Sobibor, Treblinka, Belzec et Auschwitz-Birkenau. Ce mémorial, réalisé par Stanley Saitowitz/Natoma Architects (1991), a pu être érigé grâce à l'action d'une groupe de rescapés des camps nazis venus s'installer à Boston pour y mener une nouvelle vie et grâce à l'apport financier de quelque 3000 donateurs.

ホロコースト記念碑
　ホロコースト記念碑はフリーダム・トレイルの名所の一つだ。この**6つのガラスの塔**は、ホロコーストで犠牲になった600万人のユダヤ人と、マイダネック、ケルムノ、ソビボール、トレブリンカ、ベルゼック、アウシュヴィッツ＝ビルケナウの6つのナチ強制収容所を象徴している。強制収容所で生き残ったボストン在住の一部の市民の運動が実現し、スタンリー・サイトヴィッツ／ナトマ設計事務所が1991年に建造した。この記念碑建築には3000を越す団体や個人が資金を提供した。

BEACON HILL

The hill takes its name from the signal fire (*beacon*) installed there to warn the citizenry of enemy attacks. The area, which was built up mainly in the 18th and 19th centuries, preserves so much of its original character that time seems to have stopped on **Acorn Street**, **Chestnut Street**, and **Mount Vernon Street**. The sumptuous buildings that house public institutions as well as some of the homes of the city's most illustrious figures are open to visitors: the **State House** and the **Boston Athenaeum**, the opulent **Harrison Gray Otis House** and the eccentric **Nichols House**. The city's major places of worship are also found on Beacon Hill: the magnificent **Saint Paul's Cathedral** (1820), **Vilna Shul**, the city's oldest synagogue, and the splendid **Park Street Church** (1809), defined by **Henry James** as "the most impressive mass of brick and mortar in America."

Der Hügel heißt nach dem Signalfeuer (*beacon*), das dort die Bürgerschaft vor feindlichen Überfällen warnen sollte. Das Gebiet wurde vor allem im 18. und 19. Jh. bebaut, davon hat sich so viel erhalten, dass man meint, in **Acorn**, **Chestnut** und **Mount Vernon Street** sei die Zeit stehen geblieben. Die eindrucksvollen Bauwerke dienen öffentlichen Institutionen oder sind zu besichtigende Residenzen berühmter Persönlichkeiten der Stadtgeschichte. Dazu zählen im Einzelnen das **State House**, das **Boston Athenaeum**, das prächtige **Harrison Gray Otis House** und das exzentrische **Nichols House**. Auch die wichtigsten Sakralgebäude der Stadt befinden sich hier, die großartige **Saint Paul's Cathedral** (1820), **Vilna Shul**, die älteste Synagoge Bostons und die **Park Street Church** (1809), die **Henry James** als „Amerikas eindrucksvollste Masse aus Ziegeln und Mörtel" bezeichnete.

Cette colline doit son nom au *beacon*, phare d'où un feu donnait l'alarme en cas d'attaque. Ce vieux quartier, datant pour la plupart des XVIIIe et XIXe siècles, a si bien conservé son aspect originel que le temps semble s'être arrêté dans **Acorn Street**, **Chestnut Street** ou **Mount Vernon Street**. Les somptueux bâtiments qui abritent des institutions publiques et quelques-unes des demeures de personnalités parmi les plus illustres de la ville sont ouverts au public: la **Massachusetts State House** et le **Boston Athenaeum**, l'opulente **Harrison Gray Otis House** et l'excentrique **Nichols House**. S'y trouvent également les principaux lieux de culte de la ville: la magnifique **St Paul's Cathedral** (1820), **Vilna Shul**, la plus ancienne synagogue de Boston, et la splendide **Park Street Church** (1809) dont **Henry James** écrivait qu'il s'agit de l'un des édifices en brique les plus impressionnants d'Amérique.

ビーコン・ヒル：アメリカの歴史がはじまった場所 この丘の名称は、敵の攻撃を市民に知らせるために設置された危険信号（ビーコン）に由来している。特に18世紀と19世紀に発展したこの地域は、当時の姿をよく残している。**アコーン・ストリート**、**チェスナッツ・ストリート**、**マウント・ヴァーノン・ストリート**では時間が停止したかのような錯覚を覚えるだろう。豪華な建造物の中には公共機関や町の名所が置かれ、**州庁舎**、**ボストン・アテネウム**、豪奢な**ハリソン・グレイ・オーティス邸**、風変わりな**ニコルス邸**など、一部公開されているものもある。町の大切な教会もビーコン・ヒルに建設された。壮麗な**セント・ポール大聖堂**(1820年)、最古のユダヤ教会**ヴィルナ・シュル**、**ヘンリー・ジェームズ**が「全米で最も印象的なレンガとモルタルの建物」と言った美しい**パーク・ストリート教会**(1809年)などだ。

Views of **Boston Common**: early spring snowstorm, the **Frog Pond Skating Rink**, and the **Boston's Fourth of July fireworks**.

Boston Common: Schneesturm im Frühling, der **Frog Pond Skating Ring** (Froschteich-Schlittschuhbahn) und das **4. Juli-Feuerwerk**.

Vues du **Boston Common**: tempête de neige au printemps, la piste de patinage de **Frog Pond** et le **feu d'artifice du 4 juillet**.

ボストン・コモンの眺め: 初春の雪景、フロッグ・ポンド・スケートリンク、アメリカ独立記念日のボストンでの花火

PUBLIC GARDEN

The Public Garden is of much more recent origin than the adjacent Boston Common, the first botanical garden at the corner of Charles and Beacon Streets having been founded in about 1830. The filling of the Back Bay with material excavated from Boston's hills began with the flats just west of Boston Common and created land that was laid out as a park in 1837. The fountain and the layout of the paths, the plants, and the flowerbeds all clearly show the influence of the great European gardens such as that of Versailles. The beautiful floral compositions have always provided Bostonians and visitors alike with a pleasant scenario for their strolls. During the summer the lake, which was added in 1861, is populated by geese and swans—and is navigable on the famous **Swan Boats**—while in the winter it becomes a skating rink. Standing in front of the gate on Commonwealth Avenue is the **statue of George Washington** by Thomas Ball, installed here in 1869.

Der Public Garden ist jüngeren Datums als der benachbarte Boston Common, der erste botanische Garten an der Ecke zwischen Charles und Beacon Street, welcher ungefähr 1830 angelegt wurde. Die Auffüllung der Back Bay mit Material von den Hügeln Bostons begann in den Niederungen westlich von Boston Common und ergab Landflächen, die 1837 als Park angelegt wurden. Der Brunnen, die Form der Wege, die Pflanzen und die Blumenbeete, alles zeigt den Einfluss großer europäischer Gärten wie von denen in Versailles. Die schönen Blumengruppen haben schon immer die Bostoner Bürger und die Besucher bei ihren Spaziergängen beglückt. Im Sommer bevölkert sich der 1861 angelegte See mit Gänsen und Schwänen und kann mit den berühmten **Schwanbooten** befahren werden. Im Winter dient er dagegen als Schlittschuhbahn. Gegenüber dem Parktor an der Commonwealth Avenue findet man die 1869 errichtete **Statue George Washingtons**, die von Thomas Ball geschaffen wurde.

Premier jardin botanique, créé vers 1830, à l'angle de Charles St. et de Beacon St., le Public Garden est beaucoup plus récent que son voisin, le Boston Common. L'assainissement des marais de Back Bay, comblés avec du matériau provenant des collines de Boston, commença à l'ouest du Boston Common et donna naissance à des terrains qui furent aménagés en parc à partir de 1837. Fontaines, allées, arbres et parterres: le Public Garden est clairement influencé par les grands jardins européens comme Versailles. Ses déclinaisons florales de toute beauté offrent depuis toujours un cadre de promenade enchanteur. En été, on peut aussi se promener à bord des célèbres **Swan Boats** sur le lac (ajouté en 1861) qui, l'hiver, se transforme en piste de patinage. Devant l'entrée, sur Commonwealth Av., **statue de George Washington** par Thomas Ball, érigée en 1869.

パブリック・ガーデン

パブリック・ガーデンは隣接するボストン・コモンよりも歴史は浅いものの、チャールズ・ストリートとビーコン・ストリートの間の角に1830年頃建設されたアメリカ初の植物園だ。ボストンの丘を削った土砂で川の一部を埋め立てて作られたバック・ベイ一帯は、もともとボストン・コモンの西側に広がる湿地だった。その後灌漑が行われて1837年に公園となった。噴水や小道の配置、植物、花壇を見ると、ヴェルサイユをはじめとするヨーロッパの有名な庭園の影響は明らかだ。この美しい植物園は、昔からボストン市民や観光客の憩いの場所として知られている。1861年に建設された湖は夏になるとガチョウや白鳥が群がり、有名な**スワンボート**が湖上を滑る。冬はスケートリンクに変身する。コモンウェルス大通りに向いた門の正面には、1869年にトーマス・ボール作**ジョージ・ワシントン像**が設置された。

The **Swan Boats** at Boston **Public Garden**.

Die **Schwanboote** im **Public Garden** Bostons.

Les **Swan Boats** du **Public Garden**.

ボストンの**パブリック・ガーデン**の**スワンボート**

BOSTON
COMMON
FOUNDED
1634

CITY OF BOSTON
DEPARTMENT OF PARKS AND RECREATION
THOMAS M. MENINO   JUSTINE M. LIFF
MAYOR   COMMISSIONER

The **Duckling Statue**
commemorating the popular
children's picture book Make Way
for Ducklings, *a story set in the*
Public Garden.

Die **Duckling Statue** *(Entchen-
Statue) feiert das beliebte
Kinderbuch Make Way for Ducklings,
das im* **Public Garden** *spielt.*

La **Duckling Statue** *évoque un
classique de la littérature pour
enfants, Laissez passer les canards,
dont l'histoire se déroule au* **Public
Garden**.

有名な子供向き絵本『ダクリングに道
をあけろ』を記念した**ダクリング像**。物
語の舞台は**パブリック・ガーデン**だ。

TRINITY CHURCH

Trinity Church is considered a masterpiece of the Romanesque Revival style and is certainly one of Boston's architectural jewels. Technically, it is an engineering marvel: built in 1874-77 on land reclaimed from the bay, its foundations lie on a supporting gravel layer into which 4500 wooden piles were driven to a depth of 30 feet. The state of the piles is continuously monitored for signs of rotting.

Die Dreifaltigkeitskirche gilt als ein Meisterwerk des Romanesque Revival Style (Neuromanik) und als ein Bostoner Architektur-Juwel. Sicherlich ist sie ein Wunderwerk der Ingenieurkunst, denn sie wurde 1874-1877 auf aufgeschüttetem Land gebaut. Die Fundamente ruhen auf einer Kiesschicht, in die 4500 Holzpfähle 9 m tief eingetrieben wurden. Man überprüft die Pfähle ständig auf Anzeichen von Fäulnis.

Considérée comme un chef-d'œuvre du style néo-roman, Trinity Church est indubitablement l'un des trésors architecturaux de Boston et, qui plus est, une merveille d'ingénierie. Pour la bâtir, en 1874-77, sur un terrain artificiel gagné sur la mer, on dut asseoir ses fondations sur quelque 4500 pilots de bois, enfoncés à plus de 9 m de profondeur dans une couche de gravier. L'état de conservation de ce pilotis fait l'objet d'une surveillance constante.

トリニティ教会　トリニティ教会はロマネスク=リヴァイヴァル様式の傑作で、ボストンの建造物の至宝の一つだ。最高の建築技術を駆使したこの建物は、1874年から1877年にかけて湾の埋め立て地に建築された。基部が置かれた砂利層には、木の杭4500本が30フィートの深さに打ち込まれた。この杭は腐朽の兆候がないか常に監視されている。

JOHN HANCOCK TOWER

Since 1975, the 790-foot, sixty-story John Hancock Tower, designed by the studio of **I. M. Pei**, has been Boston's tallest building. The tower was criticized for its immense size in relation to the period buildings surrounding it, like Trinity Church. But in truth, the reflections of these buildings on the shining walls of the skyscraper lend a strong dramatic accent to the panoramic effect from the nearby buildings. The 60th floor **Observatory** offers a 360° view of the city and its environs and is one of Boston's major attractions.

Seit 1975 ist der 241 m hohe und siebzigstöckige Hancock Tower, den das Studio **I. M. Pei** entwarf, das höchste Bauwerk Bostons. Man hat den Wolkenkratzer wegen seiner übertriebenen Höhe im Vergleich zu historischen Bauten wie der Trinity Church kritisiert. Aber in Wirklichkeit spiegeln sich die umliegenden Gebäude in den glänzenden Wänden des Turmes und setzen dramatische Akzente im Stadtpanorama. Vom **Observatory** im 60. Stock genießt man einen Rundblick von 360° über die Stadt und ihre Umgebung, eine der Hauptattraktionen Bostons.

Cette tour de 60 étages (241 m), due au cabinet **I. M. Pei**, est le plus haut gratte-ciel de Boston depuis sa construction en 1975. L'apparition de ce gigantesque building au milieu d'édifices anciens, comme Trinity Church, n'alla pas sans soulever des critiques. En fait, vu des immeubles environnants, le reflet des bâtiments d'époque sur les parois miroitantes de la John Hancock Tower crée un effet des plus spectaculaire. Au dernier étage du gratte-ciel, l'**Observatoire** offre une vue panoramique imprenable de la ville et de ses environs: c'est l'une des grandes attractions de Boston.

ジョン・ハンコック・タワー　**I. M. ペイ**設計事務所の設計で1975年に建造された、高さ790フィート、60階建てのジョン・ハンコック・タワーは、ボストンで最も高いビルとして知られてきた。大きすぎて、トリニティ教会などの周辺の歴史的建造物と釣り合いがとれないと酷評されたこともある。しかしこの摩天楼の壁は鏡のように周辺の建物の影を映し、そこからパノラマが広がってドラマチックなアクセントを与える。60階にある**展望台**からはボストン市と周辺地域を360度の角度から見渡せ、ボストンの観光名所の一つになっている。

BOSTON PUBLIC LIBRARY

The Boston Public Library (1848) was the first in the US to lend books to its members. The **entrance** to this neoclassical construction is surmounted by panels by **Augustus Saint-Gaudens**. Inside, the walls are decorated with murals by **Pierre Puvis de Chavannes** and **John Singer Sargent**.

Diese erste öffentliche Bibliothek in den USA lieh ihren Mitgliedern Bücher aus (seit 1848). Über dem **Eingang** zu dem klassizistischen Bau findet man Relieftafeln von **Augustus Saint-Gaudens**, im Inneren Wandgemäldezyklen von **Pierre Puvis de Chavannes** und **John Singer Sargent**.

La bibliothèque de Boston (1848) fut la première des États-Unis à accorder des prêts à ses membres. Il s'agit d'un bâtiment néoclassique dont l'**entrée** est surmontée de sculptures dues à **Augustus Saint-Gaudens** et dont l'intérieur est décoré de fresques de **Pierre Puvis de Chavannes** et **John Singer Sargent**.

ボストン公共図書館 ボストン公共図書館(1848年)は全米初の公共図書館だ。新古典様式の建物の**入口**の上には**オーガスタス・セント＝ゴーデンス**が製作したパネルが飾られている。内部の壁面装飾は**ピエール・ピュヴィス・ド・シャヴァンヌとジョン・シンガー・サージェント**が手掛けた。

PRUDENTIAL CENTER

A spectacular glass bridge links this 52-story building to **Copley Place** and the **Hynes Convention Center**, the city's major trade fair venue. On the 50th floor is the **Prudential Center Skywalk Observatory.**

Eine Glasbrücke verbindet dieses 52 Stockwerke hohe Gebäude mit dem **Copley Place** und dem Messezentrum, dem **Hynes Convention Center**. Im 50. Stock findet man das **Prudential Center Skywalk Observatory**.

Un pont spectaculaire, en verre, relie ce gratte-ciel de 52 étages à la **Copley Place** et au **Hynes Convention Center**, les deux principaux complexes commerciaux de la ville. Au 50ème étage, panorama du haut du **Prudential Center Skywalk Observatory**.

プルデンシャル・センター 52階建てのこのビルは、見事なガラスの橋で**コプレイ・プレイス**と市内最大の見本市開催場である**ハイネス・コンヴェンション・センター**に繋がっている。50階には**プルデンシャル・センター・スカイウォーク展望台**がある。

CHRISTIAN SCIENCE CHURCH

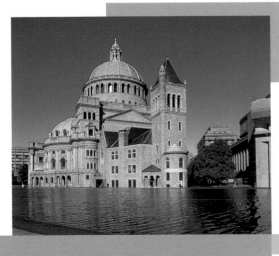

The garden, fountain, and long pool designed by **I. M. Pei** immensely valorize this important complex in the urban context.

Le jardin, la fontaine et le long plan d'eau, dus à **I. M. Pei**, mettent merveilleusement en valeur le complexe scientiste.

Der Garten, der Brunnen und das lange Becken, die **I. M. Pei** gestaltete, verleihen diesem Bau seinen urbanistischen Rang.

クリスチャン・サイエンス・チャーチ **I. M.** ペイが設計した庭園、噴水、長方形のプールなどが、市内にそびえるこの壮大な建造物を一層美しく飾っている。

Fenway Park is the oldest still-operating baseball stadium in the US (1912) and home of the **Boston Red Sox**.

Fenway Park ist das älteste noch aktive Baseball-Stadion der USA (1912) und der Standort der **Boston Red Sox**.

Fenway Park, le plus vieux terrain de base-ball des États-Unis (1912) est le fief de l'équipe des **Boston Red Sox**.

フェンウェイ・パークは、現在も使われている野球場としては全米最古(1912年)だ。またメジャーリーグの**ボストン・レッド・ソックス**のホームスタジアムでもある。

ISABELLA STEWART GARDNER MUSEUM

The Isabella Stewart Gardner Museum is one of the world's outstanding examples of the "museum-home." Created by Isabella Stewart (New York, 1840-1924), who donated her home and her extraordinary art collection to the City of Boston, the collection includes such masterpieces as *The Rape of Europa* by **Titian** and *Hercules* by **Piero della Francesca**, as well as Gothic wall hangings and Renaissance fireplaces that once adorned the homes of noble European families.

Cette demeure-musée est l'une des plus belles qui soient au monde. Créé par Isabella Stewart (New-York, 1840-1924), qui fit don de sa propriété et de son extraordinaire collection d'œuvres d'art à la ville de Boston, ce musée possède de nombreux chefs-d'œuvre tels que *l'Enlèvement d'Europe* du **Titien** et *Hercule* de **Piero della Francesca**. Dans les pièces, se trouvent des tapisseries flamandes et des cheminées Renaissance qui ornaient jadis des châteaux européens.

Das Isabella Stewart Gardner Museum ist ein herausragendes Beispiel für ein "Museumshaus". Es wurde von Isabella Stewart (New York, 1840-1924) geschaffen, die dann ihr Haus und ihre Kunstsammlung der Stadt Boston schenkte. Zur Sammlung gehören Meisterwerke wie der *Raub Europas* von **Tizian** und der *Herkules* von **Piero della Francesca**, außerdem gotische Wandbehänge und Kamine aus der Renaissance, die einst die Paläste europäischer Adelsfamilien schmückten.

イザベラ・ステュワート・ガードナー美術館　イザベラ・ステュワート・ガードナー美術館は「私邸美術館」の優れた例として世界的に有名だ。イザベラ・ステュワート(ニューヨーク生れ、1840-1924年)が創設したこの美術館は、彼女がボストン市にその邸宅と美術品コレクションを寄贈したことで誕生した。収蔵作品の中には、**ティツィアーノ**のエウロペの略奪や**ピエロ・デラ・フランチェスカ**のヘラクレス、かつてヨーロッパ貴族の宮殿を飾っていたゴシック様式の壁掛けやルネッサンス時代の暖炉などもある。

MUSEUM OF FINE ARTS

One of the oldest art museums in the US, the Museum of Fine Arts, Boston is distinguished by its important collection of **American art**, with works by **Sargent**, **Stuart**, and Boston native **Copley**. The outstanding collections of **Japanese and Indian art** are especially valuable and among the world's most complete. Alongside the collection of **ancient art** are masterpieces of the Renaissance and the Baroque (**Tintoretto, Donatello, Turner, Poussin, Velasquez**), Impressionism (**Monet, Renoir, Pissarro, Cassat**), and contemporary art (**Picasso, Clemente, Hopper, Hockney**). The prints and drawings collection is truly extraordinary, with invaluable works by **Dürer, Rembrandt,** and **Goya.**

Das Museum of Fine Arts in Boston, eines der ältesten Kunstmuseen Amerikas, besitzt eine reiche Sammlung **amerikanischer Kunst** mit Werken von **Sargent**, **Stuart** und dem in Boston geborenen **Copley**. Die Sammlungen **japanischer und indischer Kunst** sind besonders wertvoll und gehören weltweit zu den vollständigsten. Neben der Sammlung **antiker Kunst** gibt es Meisterwerke der Renaissance und des Barock (**Tintoretto, Donatello, Turner, Poussin, Velasquez**), Impressionisten (**Monet, Renoir, Pissarro, Cassat**) und zeitgenössische Kunst (**Picasso, Clemente, Hopper, Hockney**). Die Sammlung der Stiche und Zeichnungen mit Arbeiten von **Dürer, Rembrandt** und **Goya** ist von unschätzbarem Wert.

Le musée des Beaux-Arts de Boston, qui est l'un des plus vieux des États-Unis, se distingue par sa collection exceptionnelle de **peinture américaine**, avec des œuvres de **Sargent**, **Stuart** et **Copley**, artiste originaire de Boston. Remarquables, ses collections d'**art japonais et indien** sont parmi les plus complètes au monde. Outre l'**art antique**, ce musée présente des chefs-d'œuvre de la peinture Renaissance et baroque (**Tintoret, Donatello, Turner, Poussin, Velasquez**), impressionniste (**Monet, Renoir, Pissarro, Cassat**) et contemporaine (**Picasso, Clemente, Hopper, Hockney**). Quant à sa section dessins et estampes, véritablement extraordinaire, elle inclut des œuvres inestimables de **Dürer, Rembrandt** et **Goya.**

Mercenary Love by Hendrick Terbrugghen (1588-1629). Two examples of Asian and European sculpture.

Käufliche Liebe von Hendrick Terbrugghen (1588-1629). Zwei Beispiele asiatischer und europäischer Skulptur.

L'Amour mercenaire par Hendrick Terbrugghen (1588-1629). Deux exemples de sculpture asiatique et européenne.

欲愛ヘンドリック・テルブルッヘン (1588-1629)の作品 アジア彫刻とヨーロッパ彫刻から2点

ボストン美術館
全米で最も古い歴史を誇る美術館の一つで、**サージェント、スチュアート**、ボストン生まれの**コプレイ**など重要な**アメリカ美術**コレクションが特徴だ。日本美術やインド美術の収蔵品も充実し、世界的トップレベルを誇る。古代美術コレクションの横には、ルネッサンスやバロックの傑作(**ティントレット、ドナテッロ、ターナー、プッサン、ヴェラスケス**)、印象派(**モネ、ルノワール、ピサロ、カッサト**)、現代美術(**ピカソ、クレメンテ、ホッパー、ホックニー**)などの作品が並んでいる。**デューラー、レンブラント、ゴヤ**の傑作を含む版画絵画部門は必見だ。

The **Zakim Bunker Hill Bridge** (2003) and the **Weeks Footbridge** (1926) over the Charles River.

Die **Zakim Bunker Hill Bridge** (2003) und die **Weeks Footbridge** von 1926 über den Charles River.

Le **Zakim Bunker Hill Bridge** (2003) et le **Weeks Footbridge** (1926) sur la Charles River.

チャールズ川に架かる**ゼキム・バンカー・ヒル橋**(2003年)と**ウィークス歩道橋**(1926年)

CHARLES RIVER

The **Charles River** separates Boston from **Cambridge** and **Charlestown**. Its banks are lined with prestigious scientific centers and universities, such as the **Massachusetts Institute of Technology, Harvard® University,** and the **Museum of Science.** In the 19th century, a great park system was created under the direction of expert landscapers like **Olmsted,** designer of New York's Central Park. Today the **Esplanade,** the strip of green that runs along the bank of the Charles River on the Boston side, is one of the most pleasant park areas in the city: great for jogging, and the public sailing facility on the bank is always crowded. Every summer, the **Hatch Memorial Shell,** the open-air stage on the Esplanade, offers an excellent playbill of theater pieces and concerts.

Der **Charles River** trennt Boston von **Cambridge** und **Charlestown.** An seinen Ufern reihen sich bedeutende wissenschaftliche Institutionen und Universitäten wie das **Massachusetts Institute of Technology,** die **Harvard® University** und das **Museum of Science.** Im 19. Jh. wurde von Landschaftsarchitekten wie **Olmsted,** der den Central Park in New York gestaltete, ein Parksystem angelegt. Heute ist die **Esplanade,** der Grünstreifen längs des Charles River am Bostoner Ufer, ein liebliches Parkgebiet, das sich gut für Jogging eignet und im Sommer sind die öffentlichen Einrichtungen für den Segelbetrieb immer umlagert. Die **Hatch Memorial Shell** am Esplanade ist eine Bühne unter offenem Himmel, mit einem ausgezeichneten Sommerprogramm von Schauspielen und Konzerten.

Cette rivière qui sépare Boston de **Cambridge** et **Charlestown** est jalonnée d'universités et d'instituts scientifiques aux noms prestigieux tels que le **Massachusetts Institute of Technology,** l'**université d'Harvard®** ou le **Museum of Science.** Au XIXe siècle, un grand ensemble de parcs fut créé sur ses berges sous la direction d'architectes paysagistes comme **F. L. Olmsted** à qui New-York doit Central Park. De nos jours, l'**Esplanade,** la bande de verdure qui longe Charles River côté Boston, est l'une des zones aménagées les plus agréables de la ville. Elle est appréciée des amateurs de jogging et de voile, très nombreux sur les pontons. En été, sa scène de spectacles en plein air, **Hatch Memorial Shell,** propose un excellent programme de pièces de théâtre et de concerts.

チャールズ川
チャールズ川はボストンを**ケンブリッジ**と**チャールズタウン**から隔てる川で、その岸辺には**マサチューセッツ工科大学、ハーヴァード大学、科学博物館**など有名な科学研究所や大学が並んでいる。19世紀に入ってニューヨークのセントラル・パークを設計した**オルムステッド**を筆頭にする環境設計専門家の指導の下で、巨大な敷地の上に公園が整備された。今日チャールズ川のボストン側では、岸辺に沿って細長い緑地帯**エスプラネード**が伸び、市民の憩いの場所として最も人気がある。ジョギングに最適で、土手の公共の船はいつも混み合っている。毎年夏になると、エスプラネードに設置された野外ステージ**ハッチ・メモリアル・シェル**では、演劇からコンサートまで盛りだくさんの催し物が行われる。

HARVARD® UNIVERSITY

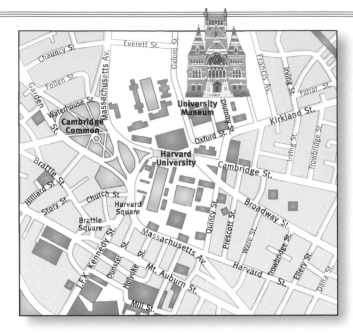

🇺🇸 Harvard® University is the oldest institution of higher learning in the US, having been founded by the local authorities in 1636. Three years later, it took the name of Harvard® College in honor of its first benefactor, **John Harvard**, a Puritan minister from London who left the college his library and half his estate. Since then, the university has turned out 40 Nobel Prize winners and 7 American Presidents.

🇩🇪 Die Harvard®-Universität, die älteste Hochschule der Vereinigten Staaten, wurde bereits 1636 gegründet. Drei Jahre später erhielt sie den Namen Harvard® College zu Ehren ihres ersten Wohltäters, des puritanischen Geistlichen **John Harvard** aus London, der dem College seine Bibliothek und die Hälfte seines Grundbesitzes überließ. An der Universität studierten 40 Nobelpreisträger und 7 amerikanische Präsidenten.

🇫🇷 L'université d'Harvard® est le plus ancien établissement d'enseignement supérieur des États-Unis. La toute première école fut fondée en 1636 par les autorités locales. Elle prit, trois ans plus tard, le nom de Harvard® College en hommage à son premier bienfaiteur, **John Harvard**, pasteur puritain londonien qui lui légua sa bibliothèque et la moitié de sa propriété. Depuis sa création, Harvard a formé quelque 40 lauréats du Prix Nobel et 7 présidents des États-Unis.

⚫ ハーヴァード大学 (Harvard® University)
ハーヴァード大学は、1636年マサチューセッツ植民地と州会議の投票で創設された、全米で最古の高等教育機関だ。その3年後、ロンドン出身の清教徒の牧師で最初の出資者である**ジョン・ハーヴァード**に因んでハーヴァード・カレッジと改名された。彼は学校に個人の図書館と屋敷の半分を寄贈した。以来ハーヴァード大学からは、ノーベル賞受賞者40人、合衆国大統領7人が誕生している。

JOHN HARVARD STATUE

The statue of John Harvard is also called the "statue of the three lies," since everything in its inscription "John Harvard, Founder, 1638" is false. The person portrayed is not John Harvard (of whom no portraits exist) but rather a model hired by the sculptor Daniel Chester French in 1884. John Harvard was not the founder of the school, and the year of its founding was 1636. Thousands of tourists visit this statue every year—and they scrape their shoes on it, a gesture said to bring luck.

🇩🇪 Die John Harvard-Figur nennt man auch die „Statue der drei Lügen", denn die Inschrift „John Harvard, Founder, 1638" enthält drei Fehler. Die dargestellte Person kann nicht John Harvard sein, von dem es kein Porträt gibt, sondern nur ein willkürliches Modell des Bildhauers Daniel Chester French (1884). John Harvard gründete die Universität nicht und die Gründung erfolgte bereits 1636. Tausende besichtigen jedes Jahr das Denkmal und scharren mit ihren Schuhen an ihm, was Glück bringen soll.

🇫🇷 Ce monument, sculpté par Daniel Chester French en 1884, est surnommé la "Statue des trois mensonges". En effet, l'inscription sur son socle – John Harvard, fondateur, 1638 – est triplement fausse. Il ne s'agit pas de John Harvard, dont il n'existe aucun portrait, mais d'un modèle et John Harvard n'est pas le fondateur de l'école, laquelle date en fait de 1636. Quoi qu'il en soit, ce monument attire chaque année des milliers de visiteurs dont certains n'hésitent pas à s'y frotter les pieds: on dit que cela porte chance.

🇯🇵 ジョン・ハーヴァード像は『３つの嘘の像』とも呼ばれている。碑文に刻まれた「ジョン・ハーヴァード、創設者、1638年」の内容総てが嘘だからだ。この彫像のモデルはジョン・ハーヴァードではなく(彼の肖像はどこにも存在しない。)、1884年にこの作品を手掛けた彫刻家ダニエル・チェスター・フレンチがどこかで見つけてきたモデルだ。第２にジョン・ハーヴァードは学校の創設者ではない。第３に創設年は1636年だ。毎年この彫像を見に来る多くの観光客が、幸運の印に靴をこの像にこすり付ける。

MASSACHUSETTS INSTITUTE OF TECHNOLOGY (CAMBRIDGE)

🇺🇸 Founded in 1865, **MIT**® is one of America's most prestigious universities, which in the 20th century won worldwide fame as a leading center for research and education. The university counts myriad academic departments in five broad categories (science, engineering, architecture, economics, and the humanities) as well as many centers for interdisciplinary research such as the famous **Media Laboratory**, where many of today's computer science technologies were developed. The **MIT**® **Museum** offers visitors an array of permanent exhibits, including the Hart Nautical Collection, the foremost of its kind in the US.

🇩🇪 Das 1865 gegründete **MIT**® ist eine der berühmtesten Universitäten, die sich im 20. Jh. als Forschungsinstitution weltweiten Ruhm erwarb. Die zahlreichen akademischen Abteilungen gehören fünf Fakultäten an, Naturwissenschaft, Ingenieurwesen, Architektur, Wirtschaftswissenschaft und Geisteswissenschaft. Außerdem gibt es interdisziplinäre Forschungszentren wie das berühmte **Media Laboratory**, in dem vieles der heutigen Computer-Technology entwickelt wurde. Das **MIT**® **Museum** bietet dem Besucher mehrere ständige Ausstellungen, darunter auch die Hart Nautical Collection, die in ihrer Art in den USA erstrangig ist.

🇫🇷 Fondé en 1865, le **MIT**® est l'une des plus prestigieuses universités américaines. Il s'est forgé au cours du XXe siècle une réputation mondiale d'excellence dans les domaines de l'enseignement et de la recherche. Le MIT® comprend une multitude de départements académiques répartis en cinq grandes branches – sciences, ingénierie, architecture, économie et sciences humaines – ainsi que plusieurs centres de recherche interdisciplinaire, comme le célèbre **Media Laboratory** où furent mises au point nombre des technologies informatiques actuelles. Le **musée du MIT**® propose une série d'expositions permanentes, dont la Hart Nautical Collection (maquettes de bateaux), la plus importante collection du genre aux États-Unis.

🇯🇵 マサチューセッツ工科大学 (ケンブリッジ)　1865年に創設された**マサチューセッツ工科大学 MIT**®は全米屈指の名門大学で、20世紀に入って時代の先端を行く研究及び教育機関として世界的な名声を博した。大学は５つの大きな分野に分かれ(科学、工学、建築学、経済学、人文学)、その中に無数の学部がある。また現在の人工知能テクノロジーの多くが開発された有名な**メディア・ラボ**など、複数の学問分野にまたがる研究所も数多い。**MIT**® **博物館**では、この分野では全米一を誇るハート・ナウティカル・コレクションなどの常設展示が行われている。

BOSTON LIGHT

On **Little Brewster Island**, facing the port, is the Boston Lighthouse, the first to be built in the United States and the last to have surrendered to automation. The original lighthouse was built in 1716. During the Revolution, the Patriots removed the torches to prevent the British ships from being guided into harbor by their light; the British army destroyed the lighthouse when they retreated in 1776. Today's lighthouse tower was built in 1783 and was raised to its present height of 89 feet in 1859.

Auf dem **Little Brewster Island** gegenüber dem Hafen steht das Boston Lighthouse, der erste Leuchtturm der Vereinigten Staaten (1716 errichtet) und der letzte, den man automatisierte. Während des Unabhängigkeitskrieges entfernten einige Patrioten die Fackeln, um zu verhindern, dass die britischen Schiffe durch ihr Licht in den Hafen geleitet würden. Die britischen Truppen zerstörten den Leuchtturm, als sie sich 1776 zurückzogen. Der jetzige Leuchtturm wurde 1783 gebaut, 1859 erhöhte man ihn auf die heutigen 30 m.

Le phare de Boston se trouve sur **Little Brewster Island**, îlot situé en face du port. Il s'agit du premier phare construit aux États-Unis, en 1716, et du dernier à avoir cédé à l'automatisation. Pendant la Révolution américaine, pour éviter que sa lumière ne guide les navires britanniques vers leur port, les patriotes de Boston en retirèrent les torches. Détruit par l'armée britannique lorsqu'elle évacua la ville en 1776, il fut reconstruit en 1783 et atteignit sa hauteur actuelle (30 m) en 1859.

Lexington Minute Man Statue recalling the American Revolution.

Lexington: die Minute Man Statue (Infanteristen-Denkmal) erinnert an den Unabhängigkeitskrieges.

Lexington: Minute Man Statue, statue de milicien commémorant la Révolution américaine.

アメリカ革命を偲ばせる**レキシントン・ミニットマン像**

ボストン灯台
ボストン港の真向かいにある**リトル・ブリュスター島**にはボストン灯台がたつ。アメリカで最初に建設されたこの灯台は、自動操作化に踏み切った最後の灯台でもある。オリジナルの灯台建物は1716年に建造された。独立革命中、ボストン湾に英国船が入り込まないよう、愛国者たちは灯台の灯りを取り外した。1776年、英国軍は撤退時に灯台を破壊した。現在の灯台は1783年に再建されたもので、1859年の増築で89フィート(30 m)という現在の高さになった。

The **Old North Bridge** in the **Minuteman National Historical Park**, theater of the battles of **Lexington** and **Concord** on 19 April 1775.

Die **Old North Bridge** im **Minuteman National Historical Park**, dort wo am 19. April 1775 die Schlachten von **Lexington** und **Concord** stattfanden.

L'**Old North Bridge**, pont historique du **Minuteman National Historical Park**, théâtre des batailles de **Lexington** et **Concord** le 19 avril 1775.

ミニットマン国立歴史公園内のオールド・ノース橋、1775年4月19日**レキシントン=コンコード**の戦いの舞台となった。

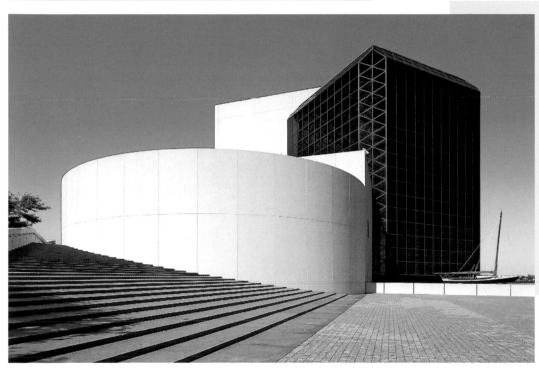

J.F.K. Presidential Library & Museum in Dorchester, **Columbia Point.**

J.F.K. Presidential Library & Museum (Kennedy-Bibliothek und Museum) in Dorchester, **Columbia Point.**

Dorchester, **Columbia Point**: le *J.F.K. Presidential Library & Museum*.

ドーチェスターの **J.F.ケネディ大統領図書館及び博物館**

South Boston: the **Convention and Exhibition Center**, one of the US's finest.

South Boston: das **Convention and Exhibition Center** (Versammlungs- und Ausstellungszentrum), eines der feinsten seiner Art.

South Boston: le **Convention and Exhibition Center**, un des plus beaux palais des congrès des États-Unis.

サウス・ボストン:全米で最大級のコンヴェンション＆エグジビション・センター

🇯🇵 **目次**

© Copyright by Casa Editrice Bonechi - via Cairoli 18/b Florence - Italy – Printed in Italy by Centro Stampa Editoriale Bonechi